Don Kennedy

Don Kennedy

# Great Sports Humor

# Great Sports Humor

*(Abridged Edition)*

## By Mac Davis

**Illustrations by**
**ROY McKIE and ARNOLD SPILKA**

GROSSET & DUNLAP • Publishers • NEW YORK

1974 PRINTING
ISBN: 0-448-11529-8 (Trade Edition)
ISBN: 0-448-13158-7 (Library Edition)

Library of Congress Catalog Card No. 73-823

Abridged Grosset & Dunlap edition, 1973

This book is dedicated to
a favorite pair of young in heart
Nancy and Bob Schantz
who are tops in my league because
of their gift for laughter.

# INTRODUCTION

Ever since the beginning of recorded sports history, there's been no letup in the flow of sports humor. And endless wealth of laughs have been mined out of the serious world of sports.

This book now invites you to a "sock-it-to-me" laugh-in with the funniest sport stories ever heard. You don't have to know a home run from a touchdown, or root for anybody, to laugh at this sprightly collection of funny stories, hilarious anecdotes, sense and nonsense, and gems of wit and half-wit. You can start this book at the end, the beginning, or the middle, and it will make for enjoyable reading in all directions. It's fashioned to delight sports fans of every age.

Between the covers of this book are to be found the champions, the also-rans, the heroes, the big shots, the little guys, the clowns, the buffoons, the famous, and the forgotten.

I've shaken the most·rollicking humor out of baseball, football, boxing, track, golf, basketball, tennis, fishing, hunting—name the sport and it's a sure bet there's a funny story from it to make you chuckle or laugh out loud. These tales are the folklore of sports.

MAC DAVIS

Although wonderful Willie Mays was the most spectacular and per-haps the greatest center fielder in major league history, he also was one of the most modest and good-natured ballplayers who ever lived. The only time during his fabulous career that the sweet-tempered "Say, Hey Kid" came close to being nasty to another player happened years ago when the San Francisco Giants' right fielder was the bragging Don Mueller.

One day, Mays and Mueller became involved in a sharp argument over a particular outfield catch. Mueller argued that right field was much tougher to play than center. He emphasized the slanted walls and the tough rebounds in right, and compared this with the freedom of move-ment enjoyed by a center fielder.

"Believe me, Willie, you've got it pretty soft in center. You ought to try playing right field," argued Mueller.

"I'm doing it now every day," said Mays, ending the debate.

In 1968, football coach Joe Kuharich had the worst season ever ex-perienced by a National Football League pilot. His Philadelphia Eagles lost their first eleven games. One Sunday afternoon, the hapless and win-less Eagles were going even worse than usual, and coach Kuharich was bellowing at his players from the sidelines. The referee came by the Phil-adelphia bench and said:

1

"Cut out the coaching from the side or I'll slap you with a penalty."

A moment later, coach Kuharich was yelling again at his players. The ref picked up the ball and paced off a five-yard penalty against the Eagles.

Now furious, coach Kuharich screamed at the ref: "Hah! Shows how much you know. That should be a 15-yard penalty."

"That's all right, Joe," said the referee soothingly. "The way you're coaching this season, five yards is plenty."

When 70-year-old manager Casey Stengel, winner of ten pennants and seven World Series championships, finally was fired by the ungrateful New York Yankees because he had grown too old, he became the manager of the newly formed New York Mets, the losingest major-league team in history. In one season alone, they lost 120 games. Oddly, manager Stengel's most popular Met star was his worst player, Marvelous Marv Throneberry. Marvelous Marv and the Mets found more ways to lose ball games than anybody thought possible—while Casey often watched in silence and suffered.

But one day, Marvelous Marv belted a terrific triple that caused old Casey Stengel to explode into the most violent verbal outburst of his managerial career. For when Throneberry reached third base, the umpire called him out for failing to touch second base. Out of the dugout came manager Stengel, roaring with rage at the ump, and the injustice of his decision. But a Met coach suddenly silenced Stengel by whispering into his ear:

"Calm down, Casey. Marv also forgot to touch *first* base!"

The famous Johnny Longden, who rode more horses to victory than any other jockey in history—6,032—tells about a priest who one day was seen blessing the nags at the race track. A bettor noticed that a long shot won after being blessed by the priest. Thereafter, he bet on every horse blessed by that priest, and he won heavily. Came the last race of the day, and the happy bettor wagered all his winnings on the horse the priest went to visit. That horse ran last. Angrily, the unhappy bettor, now flat broke, asked the priest what had happened with his blessings.

"That's the trouble with all you Protestants," said the priest. "You don't know the difference between blessings and last rites."

☆  ☆  ☆

In 1965, when Gail Sayers came to the Chicago Bears to star as their running back, he became the most sensational rookie in the history of the National Football League. He scored more touchdowns than any other grid freshman ever achieved. But early in his first season in pro football, when the Bears met the world champion Green Bay Packers, the spectacular Gail Sayers was taught a quick lesson in humility that almost frightened him to death.

He took a pitchout and confidently headed towards Willie Davis, the Packers' All-Pro defensive end. Out of the corner of his eye he could see him shaking off the Chicago blockers, and when Sayers tried to turn the corner and go upfield, the Packers' mighty linebacker Ray Nitschke barreled in alongside of Willie Davis. Rookie Sayers hit them, and the next thing he knew he was actually about four feet off the ground, with Willie Davis holding his left leg and Nitschke his right leg. Then he heard Davis say joyfully:

"Okay, Ray, make a wish, baby!"

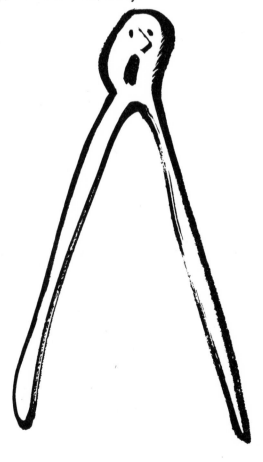

When Lyndon B. Johnson was the President of the United States, his favorite football story was about the football player from Texas University who came to the nation's capital to be interviewed by the Washington Redskins of the National Football League.

"Tell us what you can do," asked the Redskins' football coach.

"Well, gentlemen," said the young and eager Texas football player, "there are pluses and minuses. The pluses are—I can run 100 yards in 9.6 seconds even on a muddy field. I punt 70 yards, and I can throw forward passes more than 60 yards against the wind . . . ."

"And the minuses?" breathlessly asked the football coach.

"Well," replied the young football player, "seeing as I'm from Texas, I've been known to exaggerate. . . ."

☆　☆　☆

Arnold Palmer, who won more money than any other golf pro in history, tells about a golf player he once knew who became notorious for always moving his ball into a better playing position. When the man suddenly died, all his golf club members joined in the arrangements for a fitting funeral. Then the president of the golf club instructed the funeral director:

"Make sure you stamp the ground down hard after he's lowered into the grave."

"Why?" asked the puzzled undertaker.

"Because if you don't, he'll be trying to improve his lie."

☆　☆　☆

When Jim Ryun was a student at the University of Kansas, and the world's champion mile runner, he came to New York for a gala hotel luncheon. A frenzied crowd gathered to see and honor history's fastest miler. Following the luncheon meal and ceremonies, young Ryun was besieged by a wild mob of autograph hunters who proferred menus, postcards, napkins, and pieces of paper for him to sign. Always the modest hero, Ryun scribbled signatures as rapidly as he could without even once raising his head to see the beneficiaries of his autographs.

His mother, who was there, impishly thought she would fool her famous son, and get an autograph of her own. She joined the long line of autograph hunters, and some minutes later, she shoved a slip of paper in front of Jim Ryun, who did not seem to notice her as he signed it. He scrawled something and returned the paper to Mrs. Ryun without looking at her. Chuckling, she moved off, and deposited the piece of paper in her purse for safekeeping. She did not see what her son had written until she had returned to the family home in Wichita, Kansas. When she finally read what he had written for her autograph, it caused her to laugh. For Jim Ryun had scribbled on her piece of paper:

"Gosh, mom, send more cookies when I get back to school."

☆ ☆ ☆

Spectacular Bobby Hull of the Chicago Black Hawks, the only player in National Hockey League history to score 54 goals in a single season, once had a run-in with one of pro hockey's roughest tough guys, Eddie Shack. In a game against the New York Rangers, Hull skated into the corner of the ice in pursuit of a loose puck. But Eddie Shack streaked in from Hull's blind side and checked him into the boards with such force that it could be heard all over the arena.

Surprisingly, he helped Bobby Hull to his feet, and apologized: "Gee, Bobby, it won't happen again."

However, a few minutes later, Eddie Shack again smashed into Bobby Hull, and again he apologized. Again, the mild-mannered Black Hawk star said nothing. But the third time rough Eddie Shack creamed Bobby Hull and apologized, the ice-wonder barked at Shack:

"You're going to make me real mad if you continue doing it. Three times you've promised it wouldn't happen."

"I know, Bob, and I'm sorry," said tough guy Eddie Shack, "but you know that I always lie a little."

☆ ☆ ☆

The 1968 baseball season produced only one .300 hitter in the American League. He was Carl Yastrzemski of the Boston Red Sox who retained his batting title with a mark of only .301—the lowest batting average ever achieved by a major-league champion. When the old-time American League batting champion George Sisler was asked what he thought his batting average would be among the current crop of American League hitters, the Hall of Famer who twice had hit over .400 and wound up with a sixteen-year lifetime batting average of .340 said modestly:

"Oh, I guess I would do as well as Yastrzemski did, and hit about .300!"

"What, only .300?" asked one of his audience.

"Don't forget, young man," said the old-timer, "come March, I'll be seventy-five years old."

Was it a slip of the tongue or did he really mean it?

When a well-known big-time college football coach (who shall remain nameless) was taken to task by a disappointed alumni for his team's downfall in a surprising upset defeat, he alibied himself by blurting out:

"All of my college boys played like a bunch of amateurs."

☆  ☆  ☆

In 1966, Sandy Koufax, then the greatest pitcher in baseball, held out for a $100,000-plus salary for the new season. He was so stubborn a holdout that by the time the Los Angeles Dodgers agreed to pay him $135,000 a season—the most ever paid to a pitcher in all major-league history—he had missed the entire spring training grind.

Nevertheless, that season southpaw Koufax had the most glorious season a big-league pitcher ever enjoyed. He won 27 games, he hurled a no-hitter, he led the league in earned-run average, he led the league in strikeouts with 317, and he led the Dodgers to a pennant. He also won the coveted Cy Young Award, acclaiming him the greatest pitcher in baseball.

But when Sandy Koufax was asked if he regretted missing spring training because of his holdout battle, and if he might have achieved more if he hadn't missed spring training that season, he seriously made the most amusing understatement of the year when he said:

"I sure regret missing spring training. If I hadn't missed it, I certainly would have improved my batting average of .118!"

☆  ☆  ☆

One day, the New York Giants' football coach Allie Sherman, during one of his team's less successful seasons, was late for a football luncheon at a hotel. He darted through a revolving door with such speed that he upended an old dignified gentleman in his path who happened to be heading for the same luncheon.

"No offense, sir," apologized coach Sherman.

"You're telling me!" roared the old gaffer, who happened to be a loyal Giant fan. "That's been your trouble all year long."

☆  ☆  ☆

When Don Drysdale and Sandy Koufax of the Los Angeles Dodgers were teammates and the two highest-paid pitchers in major-league history, Lady Luck didn't always favor both of them at the same time. One day, the Dodgers played a double-header against the unpredictable New York Mets. Drysdale pitched the first game, brilliantly, but lost it in extra innings, by a 1-to-0 score. In disgust, he quickly dressed and left the ballpark to make a television appearance somewhere. Later, when he was apprised that his teammate, Sandy Koufax, had pitched a no-hit no-run game against the Mets, he asked curiously:

"Did he win the game?"

One day, the ardent golfer Dwight "Ike" Eisenhower was playing with a famous professional when he hooked three drives in a row. Utterly disgusted, he snarled: "I've spent my whole life trying to straighten out that lousy drive."

Quickly, the pro golfer dissented as he said soothingly:

"Not your whole life, General. I've heard that you've spent your life in other ways—as a great soldier, a colonel, a four-star general, then a five-star general, the head of SHAFE, the head of NATO, twice President of the United States, and also as an author of two best-selling books."

As General Eisenhower teed up for his next drive, he growled: "Any man who has spent his life the way you've described mine, surely ought to be entitled to straightening out his lousy drive."

When tough Herman Hickman was football coach at Yale University, he would become so upset at times that he would forget to mind his best Ivy League manners. One afternoon, his Yale team was locked in a fierce grid battle against its traditional rival, Princeton. Suddenly, the referee gave the signal for a costly penalty against Yale. Coach Hickman blew his top, for that penalty nullified a long touchdown run. As the referee paced off the penalty yardage, a furious Hickman ran along the sidelines yelling angrily:

"Hey ref, what team are you on, anyway? It's hard enough to beat Princeton without having the referee playing for them. You stink! You stink!"

The referee promptly slapped another penalty against Yale, and paced off an additional fifteen yards. Then he turned around, and said sweetly to the speechless Yale coach: "How do I smell to you from here, Mr. Hickman?"

The most unbelievable performance in the 1968 Olympic Games in Mexico City, was the 29-foot-2 1/2-inch broad-jump by Bob Beamon of the United States. He leaped nearly two feet farther than any human being had ever leaped before. When he touched down, following his record long jump, twenty-two-year-old Beamon kissed the ground again and again. When asked if the kisses expressed his feelings about achieving an historic breakthrough, and setting the fantastic all-time record, Beamon shook his head.

"No, that wasn't the reason," he said. "I was just happy I landed!"

The famous basketball coach Frank McGuire always had a simple solution for developing his great and winning college basketball teams. In his first year at North Carolina, one night he sat on the Carolina bench, arms folded, calmly watching his team get blown off the court, while at his side, his assistant, Buck Freeman, was frantic.

"Frank, they're killing us!" he screamed.

"I know, Buck," coach McGuire said softly.

"What are we going to do, Frank?" asked the assistant hysterically.

"Get better players, Buck," calmly said McGuire.

☆ ☆ ☆

When the immortal Knute Rockne was the most famous and greatest football coach Notre Dame ever had, his "Fighting Irish" commanded a loyalty from legions of rooters that was unmatched in the annals of college football. In proof of it, he would tell a favorite story of his Notre Dame football star who, after every game played, never failed to go to a particular priest for confession.

Since that priest was a bit absent-minded, he would chalkmark the number of sins confessed on his sleeve, in order to mete out the proper penance.

Once, that Notre Dame football star said in confession: "Father, I've done something sinful in our last game. I ran clear across the field and clipped a rival player."

"That was wrong, my son," said the priest, scribbling a chalk mark on his sleeve.

"Moreover, Father, when that player fell I deliberately kicked him in the ribs."

"How terrible, my son," said the priest. "Will you football players never learn true Christianity?" as he made four more chalk marks on his sleeve.

"And that's not all, Father," confessed the Notre Dame star. "When the referee wasn't looking, I gouged the player in the eye."

"Saints preserve us!" said the priest. "You're truly a disgrace to your fine football coach, and your college." And he chalked up several more marks on his sleeve.

"Tell me, son, what was the team you were playing when you committed your sins?" asked the priest.

"Southern Methodist," answered the penitent Notre Dame player.

"Oh, well," beamed the priest as he rubbed off every chalk mark on his sleeve. "I guess boys will be boys."

Babe Ruth's sly humor was at times as potent as was his mighty home run bat. In 1927, when he was making his fantastic home run record of sixty in only 151 major-league games, many rival batters needled him along the way to his imperishable glory. One of them was the brash Boston Red Sox third baseman, Fred Haney, a mediocre hitter.

One afternoon, in a game against the New York Yankees, Haney surprisingly hit his only home run of that season. It was a weak blow that barely sailed into the right field bleachers. Nevertheless, because of his feat, Haney preened like a pouter pigeon. At the inning's end, when he passed the greatest home run slugger of all time, he couldn't resist giving famous Babe Ruth the well-known needle.

"How d'ja like my homer, you big bum!" chirped Fred Haney. "Now you're only a lousy fifty homers ahead of me for this season."

Ruth said nothing. But when he came to bat in the same inning, he belted a tremendous homer that went clear over the center field fence. He jogged around the bases, and when he passed third base, he paused a second and said to Fred Haney:

"How do we stand now in homers, kid?"

One Sunday afternoon during a particularly rough game between the New York Giants and the Los Angeles Rams, the Giants' tough ten-year veteran Joe Morrison tried to intervene when an angry referee ejected Willie Young from the game, for roughing the Rams' fabulous Deacon Jones, and talking even rougher to the official.

Calmly, big Joe Morrison told the referee that football is an emotional game, and that his teammate Willie Young didn't really mean all he said to the offended referee.

"Sure, football is an emotional game," snapped the referee, "and I'm a very emotional man. And that's why Young is out of the game!"

You can never satisfy a basketball coach.

One day, Bob Foster, basketball coach of Rutgers University, was boasting to a rival coach about all the money that was spent to make the Rutgers gymnasium a nice place for visiting teams.

"Have you put in new lights?" asked the rival basketball coach.

"The finest and brightest that can be had," answered the Rutgers coach.

"New backboards, too?" asked the rival coach.

"Yes, the best that can be had," replied Bob Foster.

"And new baskets?" asked the rival coach.

"Certainly!" said coach Foster.

"That's very good," said the rival coach.

"Good? What's good about it? It's terrible!" the Rutgers' basketball coach shot back. "With all this darn new equipment we don't have the home-court advantage anymore."

☆ ☆ ☆

☆ ☆ ☆

When the Hall-of-Famer Ted Williams was making history with the Boston Red Sox, he wasn't the most popular player in the major leagues, especially in his home town. Whenever the "Splendid Splinter" appeared on the field, invariably he triggered a salvo of razzberries from the fans.

One afternoon, before the start of a game, Ted Williams made the mistake of emerging first from the Red Sox dugout. The moment the fans saw him, they exploded in a storm of booing and catcalls. Whereupon one of his teammates cracked:

"Look, guys! The early worm catches the bird."

☆ ☆ ☆

Billy Sunday was the only big-league player in history to abandon a great major-league career to become an evangelist. He became the most famous evangelist in the Christian world.

One day he was pouring it on before a huge and spellbound audience seeking salvation, and he roared at his listeners:

"Beware, all you sinners of the wrath to come. Beware, and find the path of righteousness, or there will be weeping and wailing, and a great gnashing of teeth!"

An old ex-ballplayer in the audience suddenly rose to his feet, and yelled: "Billy, I ain't got any teeth!"

Never ruffled nor at a loss for words, Evangelist Billy Sunday roared back: "Where you're going, teeth will be furnished to one and all."

☆ ☆ ☆

One of the greatest basketball coaches in history was Joe Lapchick. He coached college and professional basketball teams for almost four decades. Upon his retirement from coaching, he underwent surgery for a hernia. After the operation, the surgeon asked the fabulous basketball coach:

"Can you remember having been hit there years ago?"

"Every tap, Doc," said Joe Lapchick sadly, "every tap."

An oilman sportsman from Texas once came to Las Vegas to try his luck at the gaming tables. After a couple of successful sessions, the visiting sportsman from Texas suddenly came up with a toothache. So, he dropped in to see a local dentist. The dentist told him that it was only his nerves, and that his teeth were in perfect condition.

"Drill, anyway," urged the sporting oilman from Texas. "I feel lucky."

☆  ☆  ☆

A veteran National League pitcher who had outlived his usefulness as a hurler became an umpire in a minor league and almost immediately gave evidence that he was good enough to return to the majors. During the first week of the season, the reformed pitcher was handling a game from behind the plate when a batter, after taking four pitches, started for first, thinking he had drawn a walk.

"Come back here," ordered the umpire. "The count is three and one."

The batter came back raging. "You're out of your mind!" he howled. "Which one of those four pitches was a strike?"

"You know as well as I do," answered the former hurler calmly. "The one that was over the plate."

☆  ☆  ☆

Danny MacFayden, the once famous bespectacled major-league pitcher, was throwing for Pittsburgh one afternoon in a tight ball game when he suddenly ran afoul of Bill Klem, baseball's most famous umpire. Four times MacFayden had fired his best pitch at a rival batter, but Klem umpiring behind the plate had called each pitch a ball.

Seething with fury, the usually placid and gentlemanly Danny Mac-Fayden rushed to the plate, whipped off his eyeglasses, and held them out to umpire Bill Klem as he shouted angrily:

"You need these more than I do!"

The stern Old Arbitrator promptly ordered pitcher MacFayden out of the game. Just then, Frankie Frisch, the Pirates' manager, hustled to the scene. Although that Hall-of-Famer was a notorious umpire-baiter, surprisingly, he now tried to soothe the ump's ruffled feelings.

"Bill, have a heart," he pleaded soothingly. "MacFayden is a nice kid who sometimes gets a little excited. I'm sure he didn't mean what he said and is sorry for what he did!"

Bill Klem turned to manager Frisch and said: "Frank, I'm not chasing your pitcher out of the game for casting aspersions on my eyesight. It's because he was yelling loud enough for the customers to hear. It could incite a riot, and I won't tolerate such behavior."

At that moment, Danny MacFayden elbowed himself between the manager and umpire, as he loudly roared in his defense:

"I wasn't yelling to the grandstand at all, Mr. Frisch. I was shouting just in case Klem's ears are as lousy as his eyes!"

Danny MacFayden went to the showers early that afternoon.

☆ ☆ ☆

Umpires do not often bring down the wrath of league officials on their heads, but when they do it's usually for something that is pretty unusual. Take the case of Bill Summers before he came up to the big time. Bill was handling a series in a hot Eastern League race and the fans were really riding him hard. One of the rabid partisans stuck the name "Jesse James" on the harassed umpire, and it stuck all through the first couple of games of the series. Then, as Summers was coming into the park for the last game, he passed a mounted policeman in center field who was assigned to keep the kids from piling over the fence to see the game for free.

"Hey, officer," said Summers. "Do me a big favor, will you?"

"Sure, Jess—I mean, Bill," answered the cop. "What do you want?"

"Lend me your horse for a couple of minutes," said Bill. "I want to try something."

The cop dismounted and Summers climbed up on the animal's back. As he did so, his spikes caught in the tender hide of the beast, and the startled animal lit out towards home plate at full gallop with Summers hanging on for dear life. The crowd started to roar. When the horse reached the pitcher's mound, he suddenly realized the strangeness of it all and stopped dead in his tracks. Summers, however, kept going. Describing a beautiful arc over his horse's back, Bill sailed through the air and landed kerplunk on his seat at home plate. He rose slowly, brushed himself off, and faced the howling crowd.

"Jesse James has arrived!" he bellowed at the top of his lungs. "Play ball!"

When the game was over, Bill found a telegram waiting for him in the clubhouse. It was from the league president and it read, "Your wonderful entrance, Jesse, costs you exactly fifty bucks!"

☆ ☆ ☆

Ferenc Molnar, the internationally famous playwright and bon vivant, delighted in telling this one. Although he had been playing chess for years, he was one of the world's worst players. Soon after learning the game, years ago, he met the chess champion of Germany and the chess champion of Austria. He watched them play for a while and then sneered at their ability.

"I could lick both of you blindfolded," he jibed. "Even that would be too easy. I'll tell you what I'll do. I'll play simultaneous games against both of you champions. You can sit in front of your chessboards and I'll sit out in the hall. I'll play you without even seeing the boards.

15

We'll make our moves by sending each other notes. All right? I'll play white against the German champion and black against the Austrian."

So Ferenc Molnar walked out of the room. The German champion made his first move and sent Molnar a note describing it. Molnar merely copied the note and sent it along to the Austrian champion as his own first move. When the Austrian made the return move, Molnar copied that, and sent it to the German as his own first move.

At the close of the two matches, the inevitable result was that Ferenc Molnar, the novice at chess, had beaten one great champion and lost to the other.

☆ ☆ ☆

It was umpire Bill Guthrie who found the neatest way to throw a player out of a game. The batter, incensed by what he thought was a particularly bad call, flung his bat high in the air. Guthrie cocked his head to follow the flight of the bat.

"If that bat comes down," he commented casually, "you're out of the game."

☆ ☆ ☆

One of the ancient superstitions of baseball is that the player who sees a truck load of empty barrels before a game will get a lot of base hits. In the old days when the Chicago Cubs and the New York Giants (McGraw's Giants) were carrying on a fierce rivalry for the pennant, the two teams met for a crucial series. As the Giant team arrived at the ball park, a truck piled high with empty barrels went rumbling down the street.

"Oh, boy," chortled a Giant happily, "there goes a lot of hits for us today!"

Inspired by the unfailing omen, the Giants went out and slaughtered the Cubs. The next day, another truck load of empty barrels passed just as the Giants arrived for the game. It was a four-game series, and the New York players saw a truck full of empty barrels before each game. The Giants swept the series. Then, on the next day, a wizened little character appeared at the Giants' club house.

"Looking for someone?" asked a coach.

"Mr. McGraw," answered the little guy.

"He isn't here yet," said the coach. "Can I help you?"

"I want my dough," piped the little guy. "Mr. McGraw hired me to drive a truck load of empty barrels past here every day for four days and I ain't been paid yet!"

16

☆ ☆ ☆

Between the halves of a game between one university and Colgate not long ago, the band of the visiting eleven marched out on the field, played a couple of stirring tunes, and then followed its drum major until they stood before the Colgate stand. Then there was the usual shifting around of musicians as they prepared to spell out something for the Colgate fans. When the word was formed, however, it spelled CREST.

☆ ☆ ☆

☆ ☆ ☆

One of the greatest columnists in newspaper history, the late Heywood Broun, when he was a sports reporter could already turn a phrase with biting humor.

He was at ringside that memorable evening when Max Baer was butchering the 270-pound Primo Carnera. As the bloody Italian giant staggered to his feet after his eleventh knockdown, a colleague passionately moved by this gory display of ring courage turned to Heywood Broun and said:

"My, oh, my, but that big fellow certainly can take it!"

"Sure, but he doesn't seem to know what to do with it," replied the bored Heywood Broun.

The late Ring Lardner was another sports reporter who had the gift of humor with a single phrase that could tell an entire story. Once, he informed his public about a famous baseball star who had fallen in love, in these few simple words:

"He gave her a look that you could have poured on a waffle."

Another time, Ring Lardner wrote his opinion of a new big-league ballplayer thus:

"Although he is a bad fielder, he is also a very poor hitter."

☆ ☆ ☆

A famous football announcer broadcasting the final game of the 1948 season between the Philadelphia Eagles and the Chicago Cardinals for the professional football championship, informed his audience:

"There's very little time left . . . this is the Eagles' last attempt to kick a field goal . . . there it goes . . . IT'S A BEAUTY! . . . but it's no good."

☆ ☆ ☆

A famous football player from a tough league who became a social worker after graduation was teaching a group of reform school kids the fine points of the game. His final instructions were, "Remember, boys, if you can't boot the ball, you can still kick the fellows on the other side. Okay, now, let's get started. Where's the ball?"

"T' heck wid the ball!" yelled one of the little roughnecks. "Let's start playin'!"

☆ ☆ ☆

Shortly after Ted Williams broke in with the Boston Red Sox, the great left-handed hitter went into a terrible batting slump that left him as depressed and unhappy as a young man could be. To a reporter who happened to catch him deep in the dumps, the impetuous youth blurted out that he wished he could be a fireman instead of a ballplayer.

The next day, Boston faced the Chicago White Sox in Comiskey Park. When Ted came to bat, a roar went up from the crowd. The clowns in the White Sox lineup had appeared in front of their dugout dressed in firehats and were dragging after them a long length of fire hose and making loud sounds to indicate fire sirens. Suddenly the gleeful sounds changed to gasps of horror. Just outside the ball park a big lumber yard was beginning to go up in flames. As the black and heavy smoke billowed up against the sky, almost every fire engine in Chicago roared past the stadium, their sirens and bells going full blast.

As for Ted Williams, a player never known for his sense of humor,

18

when he heard all the excitement and noise going on outside the ball park, grumbled: "What a bunch of comics in this town! When they pull a gag on you here, they sure give it all they've got!"

It takes a lazy guy to figure out a smart angle in his trade. Take the pitcher who was once ordered to pass a dangerous batter in a crucial spot during a game. The hurler plunked the batter in the ribs with the initial pitch and watched him trot off to first rubbing his side. The manager strolled out to the mound.

"What was the idea of hitting that guy?" he demanded. "I told you to walk him."

"What's the difference?" drawled the pitcher. "As long as you wanted me to put him on base, why should I do it with four pitches when I can do it with only one?"

It was opening day in Chicago. The Cubs were playing the St. Louis Cardinals in the first game of a new season. But down in the Card's dugout, the star but eccentric pitcher, Paul "Daffy" Dean, lazily stretched out on the bench, yawned and sighed: "Ah sure'll be glad when this baseball season is over."

A couple of sporting pigeons were flying south from Poughkeepsie one fine June day. One of them looked down. "Say," he asked, "what's going on down there?"

"It's the Poughkeepsie Regatta," cooed the other. "I just put everything I had on Columbia!"

The bell clanged for the end of the round. Seconds, manager, trainer, leaped through the ropes and gathered around their fighter. One busied himself patching the battered man's wounds. Another sloshed water over him. Two of them fastened themselves, one to an ear, and began to pour out advice in a steady stream. The fighter nodded his understanding, kept nodding. The minutes ticked away. The warning buzzer sounded. The handlers climbed out of the ring. One second still held his man's ear. The bell for the next round sounded. The fighter started up from his stool as the second snatched it from under him. Then, as the fighter moved forward to resume the fight, the second raised his voice above the hubbub to give his boy a last piece of advice.

"And remember," he shouted, "don't get hit!"

☆ ☆ ☆

One Thanksgiving afternoon some years ago, sleepy Jim Crowley, former Notre Dame ace and coach of Fordham's football team, sat huddled in misery on the sidelines, watching a New York University eleven make monkeys of his powerful Rams. The clever passing combination of Boell and Dunney was gaining great gobs of ground on a befuddled and bewildered Fordham defense. At last, Crowley lost patience with the situation. Inspecting his bench, his eyes lit on an eager and ambitious sophomore back.

"Heck," thought Crowley to himself, "this kid couldn't do worse against that pair than the guys in there." He called the green youngster to his side and gave him careful instructions.

"Now listen," he said, "I want you to get in there and do just one thing. Don't pay any attention to anything else. Just keep your eye on Dunney. Do you understand? Never mind where the ball is, or who's got it. You just keep your eye on Dunney. Now get out there!"

The sophomore nodded and leaped into the fray. As luck would have it, his presence on the field seemed to make no difference. The Boell-to-Dunney combination continued on its merry way and the Violets scored again. Crowley blew his top.

"Go in there!" he barked to his regular halfback. "And tell that kid to come out!"

When the sophomore returned to the bench, Crowley was there to greet him. "What do you think you were doing out there?" he demanded angrily. "Didn't I tell you to watch Dunney?"

"Oh, yes, sir," replied the green young kid, "and I did, every minute. Boy, is he a swell player!"

☆ ☆ ☆

A big-time and influential gambler came to the racetrack for an afternoon of business. Minutes before the first race, he visited a stable where a 100-to-1 shot was prancing friskily in his stall.

"What's going on here?" he asked the trainer. "Is there something about this broken-down nag I should know?"

"Sh-h!" whispered the trainer to the suspicious gambler. "Don't let this dog hear you—he thinks he's the favorite."

☆ ☆ ☆

Slapsie Maxie Rosenbloom, former light-heavyweight champion and movie actor, cornered his pal, Maxie Baer, one day, and began to rib him about the licking he had taken from Joe Louis. The former heavyweight champion took the insults with high good humor.

"Kid me all you like," he said to Rosenbloom. "Just the same, I gave that Joe Louis a terrific scare."

"Yeah," nodded Slapsie, "you sure did. For a while he musta thought he'd killed you!"

They say that General Ulysses S. Grant made a trip to Scotland and accompanied his host to the golf course to see how the game was played. Setting the ball up on the first tee, the host took a terrific swipe at the ball, tore up great chunks of earth, but missed the ball completely. Again he swung, tore up turf, and missed.

The General watched carefully without comment. After the seventh miss, the General addressed his panting and exhausted host with great courtesy.

"The game seems to give one a considerable amount of exercise," he said, "but would you be good enough to tell me what the ball is for?"

☆ ☆ ☆

The two broad-beamed dames settled themselves in the grandstand on their first ladies' day visit, and beamed down on the field. "It's pretty, ain't it?" exclaimed one. "But I wish I knew something about baseball, don't you, dearie?"

"Don't worry," answered the other. "We don't have to know anything. They have a vampire who decides everything. There he is, the man in blue!"

☆ ☆ ☆

The big hitter on a certain playground team was suddenly injured and the only one who could be found to take his place in the game was the village idiot. The dimwit came to bat in the last of the ninth, the score tied, bases full, and the home club needing four runs to win. As the pitch came up to the plate, the dope struck out his bat blindly, connected, and drove the ball far over the distant fence. Instead of lighting out for first, he stood stockstill at the plate, a look of consternation and confusion on his homely face.

"Run, you dummy!" screamed the captain of the team. "Run!"

The dummy pulled himself together stoutly. "I will not," he said calmly. "What for? I'll just buy you fellows another ball."

☆ ☆ ☆

It seems odd that the expression "the real McCoy," meaning "the genuine article," is derived from the name of that most unusual and bizarre of boxing champions, Kid McCoy. The kid was mean and cruel in the ring, charming and attractive outside, a killer, lover, ex-convict, swindler, and finally a suicide in obscure circumstances. That's a lot of things for a great fighting champion to be, but Kid McCoy was all of them, and funny to boot. Take the origin of the expression referred to above. When McCoy was in retirement and running a saloon in midtown New York, a loud-mouthed drunk staggered into the place one evening, made the bar in two lurches and a leap, and landed next to a quiet-looking chap.

"My name's Brown," he hiccuped. "What's yours?"

"McCoy," answered the quiet man.

"*The* McCoy?" asked the lush. "You're a liar!"

After the guy was pried loose from a cuspidor, he came to his feet, a blissful smile on his battered face. "Wow!" he exclaimed. "I'll say you're the real McCoy!"

☆ ☆ ☆

The rookie didn't want his manager to know he had anything the matter with him for fear of being sent back to the minors, so he waited until he got back to the hotel where he confided in the room clerk.

"A cold in the chest?" said the room clerk sympathetically. "Tell you what you do. Go on up to your room, jump into bed, and I'll send you up something. It's a little old-fashioned, but it'll make you feel nice and warm inside."

The clerk called the hotel kitchen and asked the chef to prepare an enormous pancake and send it up, as hot as possible, to the rookie to hold on his chest.

A few minutes later, a call came from the rookie to the chef asking for another pancake, and then a second, a third, a fourth, a fifth. The chef notified the room clerk and the clerk called the rookie back.

"Are you feeling a little better?" asked the clerk cautiously.

"Oh, I feel a lot better," replied the youngster with enthusiasm, "only, could you send up a little butter and syrup with the next one?"

☆ ☆ ☆

When Casey Stengel was manager of the daffy Brooklyn Dodgers, every day was a trying day—and there was never a dull day for Casey.

An incident which helped gray poor Casey Stengel's hair in those dear old daffy Dodger days was this one involving the hard-hitting second baseman, Tony Cuccinello. Cooch laid into a fat pitch one day and sent it on a line against the center-field concrete. Casey, who was coaching at third, saw a fine rally in the making and signalled frantically to Tony to come on. The batter rounded first in high gear, passed second, and lit out for third. Casey put down his hands indicating that Tony should slide into the bag. The runner would have made it by a comfortable margin, had he obeyed instructions, but he came into the bag relaxed and standing, and the third baseman slapped the ball on him to bring the promising rally to an abrupt close. Casey let out an agonized screech and grabbed Cuccinello by the throat.

"You big bum!" he screamed. "What's the idea of coming in like that? Why didn't you slide like I told you?"

A wounded look crossed Tony's honest face. "Oh, I couldn't, Casey," he protested, "I would have busted all the cigars in my pocket."

☆ ☆ ☆

A dear little old lady who had never been away from the country finally came to the big city to live. One morning, she met one of her apartment house neighbors. She noticed that he was not particularly well dressed and a little run down at the heels. After a few minutes she asked the man what he did for a living.

"I follow the horses," he replied. "And because you're such a nice lady, I can give you a marvelous horse for only five dollars."

The gentle-hearted little old lady looked again at her ill-dressed neighbor, dug into her pocketbook, and handed him a five-dollar bill. Tucking the bill away, the man leaned over the old lady and whispered in her ear.

"The horse I'm giving you is Gallant Glow at Belmont, and let me tell you, you've got yourself a wonderful horse for your five dollars. Be seeing you!"

That night, the naive little lady told her city-wise son what she had done.

"Mother, you were swindled!" he exclaimed in disgust. "You can be sure that's the last you'll ever hear from that man. You can kiss the five dollars good-bye!"

"I don't care," said the dear old lady. "In this little apartment, where could I keep a horse if he did bring me one?"

☆ ☆ ☆

The old sportsman went fishing one bitter cold morning, and it was only after he had unpacked his gear that he discovered that he had brought everything along with him except bait. He was about to pack up and leave when suddenly a little sparrow dropped down beside him. The old sportsman was astonished to see that the little bird had a big fat wriggling worm in its beak. He gently took the worm from the bird's mouth and cut it into several pieces to be used as bait. Then, noticing that the half-frozen sparrow was looking at him with a pitiful expression in its eyes, he dug out his flask and poured a few life-giving drops into its beak. The bird, seemingly invigorated, flew off, and the old sportsman began fishing. A few minutes later, something landed on his shoulder and he almost jumped out of his skin with shock. Turning his head carefully, he was relieved to see that it was only his little friend back again. But this time there were three fine fat worms in the little sparrow's beak.

Mark Twain, great American humorist, was very fond of such outdoor sports as hunting and fishing. He had spent a very pleasant three weeks in the Maine woods one year and was making himself comfortable in the smoking car on the way back to New York. A sour-visaged New Englander sat down next to him, and the two struck up a conversation.

"Been in the woods, have ye?" asked the stranger.

"I have, indeed," replied Twain. "And let me tell you something. It may be closed season for fishing up here in Maine, but I have a couple hundred pounds of the finest rock bass you ever saw iced down in the baggage car. By the way, who are you, sir?"

"I'm the State Game Warden," drawled the stranger. "Who are you?"

"Well, I'll tell you, Warden," answered the startled Mark Twain, "I'm the biggest liar in these United States!"

Rube Lutzke of the Cleveland Indians was a rough-and-tumble clown of the diamond, but he had his serious moments, too. Near the end of his baseball career, he was traveling with his team on its final road trip when one night in the diner the players began showering poor Rube with lumps of sugar. At first, Lutzke took it with a grin, but as the lumps of sugar continued to pepper him from all directions, he slowly began to boil. When a lump hit him squarely on the nose, bringing a trickle of blood, he sprang from his seat in outraged rebellion.

"Why don't you dopes start acting your age?" he yelled. "I don't know who threw that last one, but believe me, when the season ends next week I'm not going to say good-by to a single one of you lugs. The innocent will just have to suffer with the guilty."

☆ ☆ ☆

John McGraw, who won ten pennants as manager of the New York Giants, was a soft touch for every panhandler in town. One day, one of the characters who used to hit McGraw regularly for a handout button-holed the famous manager.

"How about slipping me a buck for coffee?" he whined.

McGraw was in a dark mood that day and turned on the brash grifter with a snarl. "A buck for a cup of coffee?" he snapped. "Are you out of your mind?"

"Look, Mac," replied the moocher patiently, "do I tell you how to manage a ball club? Well, then, don't tell me how to panhandle!"

☆ ☆ ☆

Many years ago, when he was an outfielder for the Pittsburgh Pirates, Casey Stengel made a sensational catch that squashed a winning rally during an important game. As Casey trotted in from his position, he wowed the cheering crowd by doffing his cap and letting a little bird fly out from under it.

When Stengel was playing in the Pittsburgh Pirate outfield, he had one particular fan in the old right-field bleachers. This character loved Casey and his idol could do no wrong. It so happened that Casey had been having a lot of trouble with the Pittsburgh front office over salary differences, and settled on a contract that was none too pleasing to him. Came a day when somebody hit a hard drive that skipped between right and center field, and Stengel's worshipper rose to his feet and clamored for his hero to go get the ball. Stengel, however, only loped carelessly after it.

"Run!" implored the fan in horrified tones. "Casey, please run!"

Casey stopped altogether and turned to explain matters to his personal fan.

"I'd love to run after that ball, pal," he said, and his voice trembled with honest emotion, "but, believe me, I can't do it. They don't pay me enough to eat, and I'm weak from hunger."

☆ ☆ ☆

A certain veteran heavyweight whose face had been beaten as flat as a pancake by too many thudding fists finally managed to land a match in an out-of-town club. He rushed there as fast as he could, weighed in, and then went to a hotel for a nap before the contest was to take place. While he was snoozing, his manager was notified that the bout was off, due to an injury to the other fighter. The manager decided to let his man sleep, and tell him about the postponement when he woke up.

Soon after midnight, the beat-up old pug was awakened by a long-distance phone call from his girl. "Hello, sweetheart," she gurgled over the phone. "How did my baby make out in his fight tonight?"

The fighter pried open his bleary eyes and looked around the dim room, trying to recall what had happened during the evening hours. Then at last he sighed and answered. "Sorry, kid," he said. "I guess I got flattened again."

☆ ☆ ☆

Herman "Germany" Schaefer, the old Detroit second baseman, was the finest natural comedian baseball has ever known. The stories of his countless amusing antics, his swaggering, bragging and clowning every minute of his life as a ballplayer, will remain a joy forever in baseball lore. Here are two typical stories of this baseball troubadour.

One balmy afternoon, in a game against Chicago, Germany Schaefer was sent in as a pinch-hitter. It was the ninth inning, two were out and the Tigers were one run behind. Schaefer silenced the roar of the crowd as he came to the plate. Then in a loud voice he bellowed:

"Ladies and gentlemen! Permit me to present to you, Herman Schaefer, the world's greatest batsman, who will now give you a personal demonstration of his hitting powers."

The tough Chicago crowd gave him a terrific razzing. But hardly daunted, the amazing clown belted the first pitch into the stands for a home run. Slowly and majestically, he began to circle the bases. He slid into first—got up and roared: "At the quarter, Schaefer leads by a head!" He slid into second, bounced back on his feet and roared: "At the half, the great Herman leads by a length!" He came sliding into third, brushed himself off, and bellowed: "Schaefer leads by a mile!" Then he slid home as if his life depended on it, slowly rose to his feet, walked up to the edge of the stands, faced the amused crowd and doffing his cap, roared:

"This, ladies and gentlemen, concludes Herman Schaefer's afternoon performance. The world's greatest batter thanks you, one and all!"

☆　☆　☆

One sunny afternoon, Germany Schaefer tried to steal home. Like a runaway engine, he came puffing into home plate as the rival pitcher started his wind-up. He arrived in a great cloud of dust—but too late! The umpire jerked his thumb at the sky and yelled: "Yer—out!"

Germany, half-buried in dirt, merely raised his head and looked at the umpire. Then he bellowed:

"Didn't I knock the ball out of his hands?"

"No!" barked his nibs.

"Didn't I get here before the pitch?" asked Schaefer.

"No!" snapped the umpire.

"Mebbe the catcher missed the tag?" bellowed Schaefer.

"No!" again snapped the umpire.

Slowly, Germany Schaefer climbed to his feet, dusted himself off, turned to the stands, and doffing his cap shouted:

"Ladies and gentlemen! I've run plumb out of excuses."

After he got married, Joe Tinker, immortal shortstop of the legendary "Tinker-to-Evers-to-Chance" combination, brought his new bride to watch him play. It was her first baseball game, and the happy husband made up his mind to put on a real show for her. In the first inning he hit a pop-fly that landed in the blind corner deep behind third base and just managed to beat the throw to second by a long hard slide into the bag. A moment later, he tried to score from second on a clothesline single to center, and again just made it with a headlong slide.

At the end of the inning the shortstop leaned over the rail of the stand and beamed fondly on his little wife. "How do you like it?" he asked.

"Oh, wonderful," answered the blushing bride, "but I do wish you could be a little more graceful. You fell down twice going around the bases!"

☆ ☆ ☆

Casey Stengel was a full-fledged baseball clown in his own right, but the brand of lunacy he found in Brooklyn during his short tenure as manager of the Dodgers almost drove him crazy.

One afternoon, during an important and close game, Frenchy Bordagaray put a damper on a promising Brooklyn rally by being caught off second base despite the fact that he had hardly taken much of a lead. When the player returned to the bench, manager Casey Stengel blew his top as he angrily roared at him:

"What happened? What happened to you, you big dope? Did you fall asleep? I want to know what happened?"

Frenchy Bordagaray, without batting an eyelash, answered: "Gee, Casey, I don't know. There I was, standing on the bag tapping the base with my foot, and I guess they got me between taps."

☆ ☆ ☆

Once, when the Dodgers were in the midst of a long losing streak, Frenchy Bordagaray accidentally conked Manager Stengel on the head with a thrown ball during pre-game practice. Casey was furious, but he let the matter pass for the moment. The Dodgers won that day. After the game, Frenchy buttonholed Casey in the locker room.

"Casey," he said with dead-pan seriousness, "I think we can keep on winning if I hit you on the head every day for luck!"

☆ ☆ ☆

Before the game started, Brooklyn Dodger Manager Uncle Wilbert Robinson called all his players together in the dugout and glared at them angrily. "I'm mad now, boys," he said bitterly, "and the next one of you who pulls a rock on this field is going to be fined fifty smackers."

Then the irate but dignified little manager waddled out to home plate and handed the umpire his family laundry list—instead of the Dodgers' batting order for the day!

☆ ☆ ☆

The bookmaker suddenly fell ill and his anxious son hovered at the bedside. "Don't stand around," groaned the sick man. "Get the doctor."

The boy went off and a few minutes later a doctor showed up. After he left, the sick bookie called his son in. "That wasn't my regular doctor," he growled. "What's the idea of bringing a stranger?"

"Well, I'll tell you, Pop," explained his son. "I got to the guy you wanted and I saw that his sign read, 'Consultations 10-1.' I was just going in when I noticed that the doctor next door had a sign reading 12-1. So I got the one who offered the bigger odds, just like you always advise me to do."

☆ ☆ ☆

A couple of beginners were playing golf, or trying, and on the very first hole both of them drove deep, hard and far into the rough. Reaching the spot where the balls had last been seen, they went to work trying to find them. They were crawling on their hands and knees in the poison ivy when a nice old lady who had been standing by watching the exhibition, suddenly decided to take a hand. "Excuse me," she said feelingly. "Would it be cheating too much if I told you where the balls were?"

☆ ☆ ☆

Once, to shake the Brooklyn team out of a long losing streak, manager Wilbert Robinson asked the newspapermen to pick his lineup for the afternoon's game.

"You wise guys are always winning games for me in your newspapers," grumbled Uncle Robbie. "Now let's see you win one out there on the field."

So each baseball reporter in the press box picked a lineup. Manager Robinson tossed them all into his baseball cap, drew one out and gave that lineup to the umpire. That lineup had Babe Herman, then masquer-

ading as a first baseman, in left field. And the Dodgers went out to play the tough St. Louis Cardinals, led by the immortal Rogers Hornsby.

Miraculously, for eight innings all went well and the Dodgers managed to hold on to a slim one-run lead going into the ninth. But in the Cards' final inning, Hornsby, with two on and two out, poked a high fly to left. Babe Herman got all set to catch the ball, but it cracked down on his head and St. Louis had the ballgame.

Immediately after that game, an angry Wilbert Robinson stormed into the Brooklyn press box and roared at the newspapermen:

"Who's the crackpot who put Herman in left field?"

☆ ☆ ☆

The basketball game was in its closing minutes, and the highly regarded team from the Far West was slowly cutting into New York University's lead. Up and down the court ran the Violets, desperately trying to stave off the last-minute challenge of the opposition.

Howard Cann, N.Y.U. coach, suddenly sprang to his feet. "Plutz!" he shouted. "Where's Plutz! I want him to go in right away!"

"But, coach," piped up a substitute from the bench, "Plutz has been playing all through the game. He's in there now."

"Well, then," barked Cann without hesitation, "get him out, he needs a rest!"

A young ballplayer who had never gone very far in school finished his first major-league season in fine style and dropped in at the club offices to discuss his next year's contract.

"I'd like a raise, boss," he said. "I did pretty good this year."

"Why, certainly, my boy," answered the club owner. "How does a one-fourth raise in pay strike you?"

"One-*fourth?*" yelled the kid indignantly. "Nothing doing! After the way I played this season I ought to get at least a one-*fifth* raise!"

The club owner met his terms.

☆ ☆ ☆

Early one morning a bookie who was walking down a deserted street suddenly heard a sad voice groan. "Oh, what a lousy life this is!"

The bookie stopped and looked around him. There was no one in sight. As he resumed walking, he again heard the sorrowful voice. "Who'd ever believe this could happen to me," it wept. "Oh, me, oh, my!"

The man stopped and again looked up and down the deserted street. The only living thing in view was a weary-looking horse hitched to a wagon piled high with bananas. The bookie stared at the animal, wondering if his imagination could be playing him tricks. He was almost startled out of his wits when the horse looked him full in the eye and said, "Don't look so surprised, buddy. It's me talking, all right."

"This is incredible," muttered the bookie.

"Not at all," the horse moaned unhappily. "What's incredible is the life I have to lead—me, who once ran in the Kentucky Derby. All day long, from dawn to dark, I pull this heavy wagon full of bananas. And, what's more, the driver beats me and doesn't give me enough to eat."

"Horrible!" exclaimed the shocked bookie. "I'm going to talk to your owner right away and tell him what a fool he is. Doesn't he realize what a prize he has in you? Why, you're the only horse in the world that can talk!"

"No, no!" said the horse in great alarm. "Don't do it, please! If he finds out I can talk, too, he'll have me yelling, 'Banana-a-a-as!'"

☆ ☆ ☆

Baseball will never tire of Babe Herman stories. They are priceless in the lore of the national pastime. The Brooklyn Babe and his antics weren't fable out of fiction. Floyd Cave Herman was real—the daffiest Brooklyn Dodger of them all.

Once, the Babe cornered a baseball reporter and pleaded with the newspaper scribe to stop painting him in print as a clown.

"I know you fellas make a living writing pieces for the paper about ballplayers, but why don't you stop harping on me? I ain't no different from other players. Baseball is my bread and butter—I've got a family to support and all these crazy stories about me hurt my reputation."

Brooklyn Babe was so convincing in his little talk that the baseball reporter began to feel pangs of guilt. As the ballplayer and scribe were about to part, Babe Herman fished out a cigar butt from his vest pocket, stuck it into his mouth, and took a few vigorous puffs at it.

"Want a match to light it?" the reporter inquired.

"Naw, never mind," said the Babe walking away. "It's lit."

☆ ☆ ☆

Once, Babe Herman complained to a baseball reporter that he was fed up with all the foolish stuff written about him as a goofy clown.

"I'm no clown!" insisted the Babe. "I'm a serious guy. I read books. I wish you'd say something serious about me sometime."

"All right," said the newspaper scribe. "What do you think of the Napoleonic Era?"

A blank look spread over Babe Herman's face. He scratched his head for a moment in deep thought, and drawled without the trace of a smile:

"I think it shoulda been scored as a hit."

☆ ☆ ☆

Another Babe Herman classic is of the time when he held a press conference and made this memorable statement to a flock of reporters:

"After the season a rich friend of mine wants to take me on a trip around the world, but I told him I'd rather go someplace else."

☆ ☆ ☆

Many years ago, a famous jockey, Frank Garner, who was also notorious as a tightwad, rode Typhoon to victory in the Kentucky Derby. The jockey decided that a celebration was in order. So he invited the entire jockey colony to a dinner at the most expensive restaurant in Louisville.

About one hundred guests, jockeys, trainers, grooms, stable boys and hangers-on, all crowded into the restaurant to eat at Frank Garner's expense. When the large assemblage was seated around the tables in the swanky dining room, jockey Garner arose and shouted happily:

"Listen, friends! This is a special occasion and I want all of you to have a good time and eat well. So all of you order something fancy and extra special."

That turf crowd wasn't exactly used to eating anything fancy, so they told Garner to order dinner for everyone. For a few minutes there was a deep and expectant hush as the famous tightwad jockey studied the menu. Then he yelled at the waiter:

"Bring us one hundred dollars' worth of ham and eggs, fancy and extra special!"

When Maxie Rosenbloom was the light-heavyweight champion of the world, he loved nothing better, after a hard day's workout, than to eat well.

One day, he was told about a swanky new restaurant where they served the biggest and finest steaks in town. No sooner had he finished the day's workout than he rushed to the phone to call the fancy eating place.

"I'm Maxie Rosenbloom," announced the fighter, "light-heavyweight champion of the world. I'll be down to your place in a couple of minutes and I want the best darn steak you got. Put it on the fire now. I'll be there in a jiffy."

"And how do you like your steak, sir?" asked the head waiter haughtily.

"Well to do, of course!" shouted Maxie. "I can't stand roar meat, y'understand? And with it, I want a side order of sparrow grass with holiday source!"

☆ ☆ ☆

Speaking of spitting, there is another tale told of an ex-daffy Dodger, Frenchy Bordagaray, who during his brief tenure as manager of a Brooklyn farm club spat in an umpire's eye.

When the league president announced a 60-day suspension, Frenchy said:

"Okay, maybe I did wrong, but it's a little more than I expectorated."

☆ ☆ ☆

A hard-boiled prizefighter got himself into a jam with the authorities and was sentenced to jail for ninety days. He found himself in a cell all by himself, a situation he did not particularly care for. After a couple of days passed, he suddenly heard a rustle of sound in the corner of his cell, and discovered a frightened little mouse. He picked the mouse up in his big fist and glared at it.

"I oughta slap yer brains out," growled the roughneck. "What do ya mean comin' in here and botherin' me?" The mouse did not answer. "At least," continued the tough guy, "if you was a tough character like me, I woulda had some respect fer ya. But look at ya, yer so scared I'm ashamed to be in the same cell with ya."

Then a thought occurred to the fighter and his face brightened with pleasure. "I know what," he said to the mouse, "I'll teach ya how to be tough like me. I'll train ya to be a rough, tough critter. How would

ya like that?" And the ring badman gave the mouse something to eat from his own food and began a training program designed to make the mouse as tough as he was.

The ninety days passed quickly for the old fighter now that he had company and a job of training to do. When he was turned loose, the roughneck had the little mouse safely tucked away in his side pocket. Fighter and mouse were great pals now. And, since he had developed a considerable thirst in jail, he made for the nearest bar.

Our hero was making up for lost time when the bartender refused to serve him any more to drink. The old fighter frowned and leaned threateningly across the bar. "Whadda ya mean?" he snarled. "You put another shot of liquor on the bar or I'll pick ya up and sling ya through that wall and clean across the street!"

There was a short pause as the tough fighter took a deep breath. Before he could say another word, the little mouse poked his head out of the pug's pocket. The little fellow's eyes glared at the bartender. "And that," he screeched, "goes for your cat, too!"

☆  ☆  ☆

Two friendly but timid sportsmen had an argument. The battle of words waxed hot and furious until one of the men slapped his friend's face. The man who got slapped challenged his hot-tempered friend to a duel, and the challenge was accepted. Seconds were quickly chosen, and the two timid sportsmen agreed to fight the duel on the following morning in a secluded clearing—with pistols at twenty paces.

Came the dawn and only one of the would-be duelists showed up.

He and his seconds impatiently waited for his opponent ten minutes, thirty minutes, an hour—but no opponent. Finally, a messenger arrived breathlessly with a note from the missing man. It read:

"My dear friend, I may be delayed, but please don't wait. Meanwhile, you shoot!"

☆ ☆ ☆

The stranger had been sitting between the two chess experts for four hours without saying a word or moving a muscle. At last one of the players could stand it no longer.

"Look here, mister," he said, "you've been watching us for four hours. Why don't you go some place and play a game yourself?"

"Can't," muttered the kibitzer without taking his eyes from the board, "I ain't got the patience."

☆ ☆ ☆

Two well-known chess players vacationing at an inn sat down one morning to play a game of chess. A few moments after they had started, they were joined by the proprietor of the inn. For two hours he sat watching the two chess experts play without uttering a single word.

Suddenly, a dispute arose between those two chess masters concerning the problem of a certain move. Finally, they both agreed to accept the decision of their lone spectator. So they turned to him and asked for the inn owner's opinion.

"Gentlemen," he shrugged his shoulders, "who knows anything about chess?"

"Do you mean to say that you don't know anything about the game?" asked one of the players.

"Do you mean to say that you don't know how to play chess and yet you've been sitting here for two hours watching us?" shrieked the second player.

"But why?" both players demanded to know in chorus.

"Gentlemen, what else could I do?" replied the owner of the inn. "Did you ever see my wife?"

☆ ☆ ☆

A little Italian priest was very fond of the races and attended all the meetings he could. He never made a bet, of course, and did what he could to dissuade others from doing so.

"It's the height of folly," the priest would say to the horse players who listened to him. "Just look at me. I know every owner, every train-er, every jockey here at the track. Every time one of them has a horse he is sure will win, I get the tip. Even then, if the bookmaker thinks the horse will lose, he refuses to take the bet from me. On top of that, if the horse loses anyhow with my money on him, they refuse to accept my money."

"That's pretty cozy," said a listener. "I wish I could have breaks like that."

"Nonsense," said the priest. "So far this year, even I am five hundred dollars behind!"

☆ ☆ ☆

The late Ring Lardner wrote some wonderful stories based on the characters he met when he had been a sports writer. His famous Alibi Ike was really modeled on a rather well-known outfielder. Lardner showed this player one of his Alibi Ike pieces and the next day the an-gry ballplayer came looking for the writer with murder in his eye.

"What's the idea?" he screamed. "You can't write about me like that! I got a good mind to go out and sue you for it!"

"Hey, wait a minute," protested Ring. "You can't do that. I didn't even mention your name in the story."

"Why do you suppose I'm sore?" growled the big-headed athlete. "Nobody knows it's me you wrote about!"

☆ ☆ ☆

A couple of nervous horse players were standing at the rail watching an exciting race in which they had bet on different horses. Their two choices came down the stretch a half length or so apart and the one whose horse was trailing began to try to root his animal home.

"Get up there!" he screamed. "Go to the outside! Look out, you're going to get into a pocket! Keep going! Keep going! Outside! Outside! Look out for the hole! Look out—"

The other nervous player grabbed his friend by the sleeve angrily. "Leave that horse alone!" he yelled. "You're making him nervous!"

☆ ☆ ☆

A New York boxing manager signed up a promising youngster and ar-ranged a match for him in a small town in Pennsylvania. The boy went off to fill the engagement alone, since the manager was unable to accom-pany him.

39

The next day, a despondent young man reported to his manager. "They give the other guy the decision," he said.

"What?" howled the manager. "He should have been easy for you. What happened?"

"Ah, you know," muttered the boxer. "It was just one of them home town decisions."

"But you licked him, huh?" asked the manager hopefully.

"Sure," said the kid. "Why, the guy was all covered with blood when the fight was over."

"Covered with blood?" screamed the manager. "How could they give him the decision?"

"Beats me," said the kid sadly. "Except maybe they knew it was my blood!"

☆ ☆ ☆

Travis Jackson was a smart shortstop for the New York Giants, always on the alert to pull something on the opposition. One of his favorites was the hidden ball trick, one that works very seldom in the big leagues. But Jackson did it, and one of his most memorable was this one.

Late in the second game of a long double-header, a batter hit a double and went sliding into second a moment before Jackson received the throw from the outfield. The runner got up and brushed himself off so busily that he did not notice that the Giant shortstop had kept the ball.

"Nice hit," said Jackson as he moved away from second. Then he came back a couple of steps. "I'm half-starved," he said. "Boy, am I going to have a dinner tonight!"

"Yeah?" asked the batter. "Whatcha gonna have?"

"Steak," said Jackson. "Three inches thick, rare as can be, with French fries and fried onions."

"Fried onions?" asked the runner on second.

"Yeah," said Jackson. "Don't you like them?"

"Not fried," said the batter. "I like 'em boiled. The big ones, Bermudas, big as baseballs."

The two men had wandered away from second base together and now Jackson was between the runner and the bag. Jackson turned his glove, showing the ball in its pocket.

"Like this?" he asked.

☆ ☆ ☆

The small-time football coach with a reputation for optimism came into the locker room to give the boys a pre-game pep talk. "All right, boys," he cried cheerily, "here we are, unbeaten, untied, and unscored upon—and ready for the first game of the season!"

☆ ☆ ☆

The husband came home from a day's fishing and tossed an empty creel on a chair. His wife looked at it and then said, "Didn't you go fishing today?"

"Yep," answered the husband.

"Didn't you catch anything?" asked his spouse.

"Sure did," replied the fisherman. "Hooked a fish so big I couldn't haul it into that boat."

"What happened, then?" asked the wife.

"Heck, the darn thing pulled me right over the side," answered the fisherman.

"Then why aren't you soaking wet?" asked the puzzled wife.

"Because I landed right on the fish's back!" shouted the fisherman.

☆ ☆ ☆

Charley Gehringer, considered the greatest of second basemen, never had very much to say in the long years he spent with the Detroit Tigers. In fact, it was almost impossible to get a word out of the mechanical marvel, on or off the field. Nor did he care much to listen to anybody else make unnecessary conversation.

Gehringer roomed with the Detroit pitcher, Chief Hogsett. The two men were well matched, for the big Indian was as much of a clam as his roommate.

The two were having breakfast together one morning. A deep silence prevailed. Then the Chief leaned across the table. "Charley," he said, "please pass the salt."

Gehringer stiffened and then looked accusingly at his companion. "You could have pointed," he said, and went on with his breakfast.

☆ ☆ ☆

Charley Moran, famous as the major-league umpire who made the classic remark, "They're either safe or out, fair or foul, but they're nothing till I call them!" is just as well remembered as the coach of the little Centre College football team that came north to vanquish stunned Harvard years ago. The quarterback of that great Centre College team was the equally famous Bo McMillin, All-American in 1919 and later a fine coach himself. Bo was on the bench one day and the fans in the stands began to yell in unison, "We want McMillin! We want McMillin!"

Finally Bo sprang to his feet, threw aside his blanket, and trotted over to Coach Moran.

"Do I go in?" he asked eagerly. "Who do I replace, coach?"

"You don't replace anybody," said Charley gently. "Just go run up into the stands and join your friends. They want you more than I do."

When Bob Zuppke was coaching his fighting Illini some years ago, he loved to instill fighting spirit in his teams with fiery harangues before the games. With a bunch of untried sophomores, Zuppke was having a tough season when the Iowa game came along. There was little chance for Illinois to win, and Zuppke really poured it on in the dressing room before the game.

"This is the supreme test, men!" he boomed to the assembled squad. "Steel yourselves for your greatest effort! Get out there and be ready to die for Illinois. There'll be no one taken out of the game unless he's dead!"

Out went the raging Illini. They played themselves into the ground trying to stave off the superior Iowa eleven. Late in the game, one of the Illinois players suddenly collapsed on the field. Zuppke sprang up.

"All right, you!" he snapped at a sophomore substitute. "Go out there and replace that man!"

"Yes, sir!" gasped the startled youth. He rushed out on the field, looked down at the stricken warrior for a moment, and then came trotting back to the sideline.

"What's the matter with you?" shouted Zuppke. "Get back there on the field and take that man's place!"

"It ain't necessary, coach," answered the green sophomore timidly. "He's still breathing a little."

In 1968, the St. Louis Cardinals put up a 10-foot-5-inch bronze statue on a marble pedestal 8 feet high, in front of Busch Stadium, their home ballpark, in honor of Stan Musial, the greatest player in the history of the club. At the dedication, when that statue of Musial was unveiled, the Cards' manager, Red Schoendienst, who had been Musial's teammate

and roommate in their playing days, and had remained one of his closest and warmest friends, arose to speak in tribute to a baseball immortal. Looking at the beaming Stan Musial, he said:

"In your twenty years as a player for the St. Louis Cardinals you've done a lot for them, and for all baseball. Now you're going to give the pigeons a break."

☆ ☆ ☆

For Paul Fogarty it was the final game of his senior year, and his last chance to play in a Notre Dame game. For three long years Paul had ridden the bench, impatient and eager for his chance. Now the minutes were ticking away and Fogarty squirmed unhappily in his seat on the sidelines. Suddenly there was a tremendous pile-up on the field. The players rose slowly until all but one of them were back on their feet. Rockne sprang up, anxious and worried, and dashed out on the field to see what had happened to his stricken player. There was a moment's hasty discussion and the great coach came back to the bench, his eyes darting up and down the row of substitutes.

43

"Fogarty!" he barked.

Paul leaped to his feet. At last his chance to win a varsity letter had come! "Yes, coach!" he gasped, his heart leaping wildly in his chest.

"Get out there quick!" shouted Rockne. "O'Brien ripped his pants. Give him yours!"

☆ ☆ ☆

The immortal Knute Rockne used to hold skull sessions with his players that were as sharp and demanding of the players as any mathematical quiz. It was Rockne's custom to fling out complicated questions in strategy and demand immediate answers from his Notre Damers. One afternoon, Rockne shot out this question at his third-string quarterback: "Our ball, third quarter, second down, two yards to go and we're at mid-field. What do *you* do?"

"Me?" asked the startled third-stringer. "I just slide down the bench to get a better look at the next play!"

☆ ☆ ☆

A boxing promoter discovered at two o'clock that he was short a fighter for a card he was putting on that night. He hurried out to see whether he could find somebody to fill in for the missing fighter. On the street corner he saw a tough-looking kid.

"Hey," said the promoter to the kid. "Haven't I seen you hanging around the gym?"

"Yes, sir," said the tough kid.

"I have a spot in the preliminaries for a willing young fighter tonight. Want to fill in?"

The tough youngster hesitated. "Can I have a couple of hours to make up my mind?" he asked.

"Let me know at five o'clock," said the promoter.

Promptly at five, the tough kid reported to the promoter that he would take the fight. Later he stepped into the ring and, to everyone's surprise, knocked out his opponent in a couple of rounds. As the promoter paid him off he could not conceal his curiosity. "Tell me, kid," he asked, "what were you doing in the couple of hours you needed to make up your mind this afternoon?"

"I wasn't feeling sure of myself," answered the tough kid, "so I went out picking fights with everybody I met. Knocked off a few guys easy, so I figured I could do all right in the ring. After all, I was going in there for the first time in my life and I had to make sure I could do it!"

☆ ☆ ☆

When the surgeon got to the "consultation," he discovered that half a dozen other doctors had shown up, so it was decided to play poker instead. Our friend was having a streak of bad luck until at last he was dealt aces back to back on the first two cards in a hand of stud. His neighbor on the right picked this promising situation to suffer a fatal heart attack, slumping to the floor under his seat.

The doctors lifted the stricken player tenderly and put him on a couch. There was nothing they could do for him.

"What do we do now?" asked one of them, turning to the surgeon. "This is terrible."

"You're quite right," answered the surgeon promptly. "I suggest that, out of respect for the dead, we finish this hand standing up."

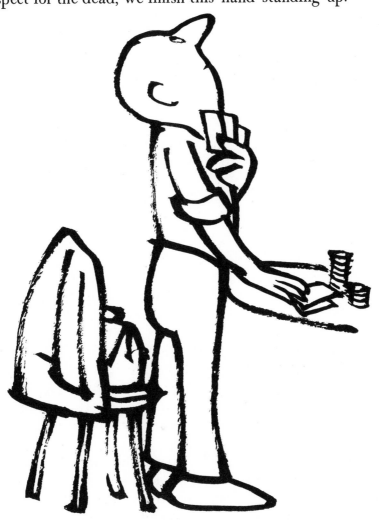

☆　☆　☆

Ben Hogan, the caddy who rose to the eminence of one of the world's greatest golfers, had a warm spot in his heart for all caddies. Whenever he played, he always tried to make his caddy feel important.

Once, Hogan found himself with a new caddy most eager to serve him. To make the boy feel at ease in the presence of golf royalty, when this famous golf champion had a difficult shot to make, he turned to his caddy and asked:

"What club would you use here?"

Without hesitation, the caddy replied: "I'd use my number 8 iron."

Ben Hogen did and was short with his shot. On the next hole, came another difficult shot, and again he asked his caddy:

"What club would you use here?"

Again the caddy replied: "My number 8 iron."

Surprised and rather amused, Hogan did and again he made a bad shot.

On the third hole, again Hogan turned to his caddy and asked him: "What club would you use here?"

Again the boy replied: "I'd use my number 8 iron."

By this time, Ben Hogan was somewhat annoyed as well as curious. So he snapped at his caddy:

"Say, what's the big idea always telling me to use the number 8 iron on every shot? Don't you know anything about this game?"

The caddy replied: "Mr. Hogan, you asked me what I'd use and I told you the truth. I'd use my number 8 iron on all shots because that's the only club I own."

☆　☆　☆

The old Brooklyn Dodgers were in the midst of a rally and Chick Fewster, who was sitting in the dugout next to Uncle Wilbert Robinson, enthusiastically grabbed a bat and began to pound away furiously on the steps in order to rattle the opposing pitcher.

"Stop that!" ordered Uncle Robbie.

Fewster looked at the eccentric rotund little manager in amazement. "Why?" he asked. "Ain't we got a rally going?"

Robbie nodded toward a corner of the Brooklyn bench where his star hurler, Jesse Petty, was slumbering soundly.

"I don't want you to wake up ol' Jess," he whispered.

☆　☆　☆

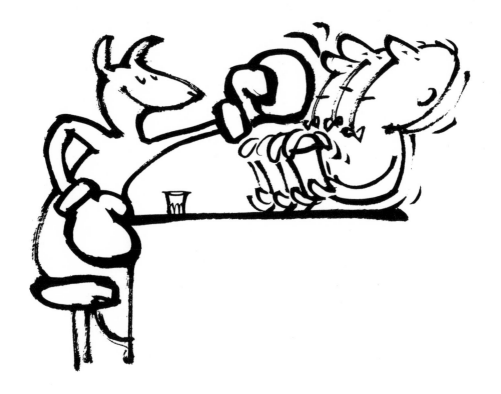

You don't have to believe it, but this boxing kangaroo dropped in at this swank hotel bar, plunked down a dollar bill and asked for a shot of Jack Daniels and soda.

"That'll cost you $1.25," said the bartender.

"Ooops, sorry," said the kangaroo, and tossed another quarter on the mahogany. He swallowed his drink and started to leave the place. The bartender leaned over the bar. "Say," he said, "we don't get many kangaroos in here."

"That doesn't surprise me," answered the kangaroo. "At $1.25 a shot, you aren't likely to see any more kangaroos!"

☆ ☆ ☆

Most sport fans are familiar with famous tennis star Don Budge's greeting to England's Queen Mary when she entered Wimbledon Stadium one day to watch him play for the championship. (If you don't, here it is: Don was already on the court, ready to serve, when he saw the great crowd rise to its feet respectfully. Since he was already standing, he waved his racquet and called out cheerfully, "Hi, Queen!")

When Jack Dempsey was heavyweight champion of the world, he vis-

47

ited England and was taken to a night club one evening. His host stopped before a table.

"Oh, Jack," he said. "I'd like you to meet the Duke of York."

Jack stuck out his hand at the man who was to become the King of England. "Stay where you are," he said magnanimously. "Don't get up for me."

Then there was Kingfish Levinsky, a somewhat different kind of heavyweight prizefighter whose exploits in and out of the ring have added so much hilarity to boxing lore. He, too, made a trip to England where he positively captivated the natives with his manhandling of the English language. When his tour came to an end, his English friends invited him to a formal banquet in his honor. As soon as the glittering guests were seated, the host rose to his feet to propose the customary toast that opens all English banquets. Only Levinsky, the guest of honor, remained in his chair.

"To the King!" cried out the host, raising his glass aloft.

"To the King!" echoed the others.

At this point, Kingfish Levinsky climbed slowly to his feet, a shy grin spread wide on his battered face. "Gee, fellas," he gulped. "Thanks a million."

☆ ☆ ☆

It was just a few minutes before the big game with Harvard, and Coach Ducky Pond was steaming his Yale boys up to a frenzy of excitement before sending them out on the field. "Remember," he thundered, "you men are playing for Yale! Y-A-L-E! And do you know what those letters, Y-A-L-E, stand for? I'll tell you! Y is for Youth, something you all have, but youth alone is not enough. A is for Ability, which added to youth may get you somewhere. L is for Loyalty, loyalty to alma mater. And E is for Effort. Put youth, ability, loyalty and effort together and it spells out—victory! Victory! Victory! Now go on out there and get them! Remember—Y-A-L-E spells victory!"

Just then the signal came to go out on the field. As they passed through the tunnel leading from the locker room, one big Blue player turned to his neighbor. "You know," he muttered, "we'd never have gotten out on the field at all if Ducky had been coaching us at Rensselaer Polytechnic Institute!"

☆ ☆ ☆

A stickler for clean play was the immortal All-American Albie Booth, but the explosive little Yale hero of yesterday got a lesson once that he will never forget. Booth was in the Yale backfield one day in a game against an inspired Georgia eleven. For the first time in his life, little Albie was finding himself tossed around most unceremoniously by an opposing team, and the chief thorn in his side was the quick-thinking All-American end, Catfish Smith. Every time little Albie took off with the football tucked under his arm, it was Catfish who dumped him harshly to the turf of Yale Bowl. Each time Booth would get up, try again, get slammed back, get up, try again, get thumped. Whichever way he seemed to turn, there was Catfish reaching for him. Some of the tackles were a lot rougher than seemed necessary, but Booth held his tongue in dignified silence as long as he could. Then, in the last quarter, Catfish Smith jarred him to his heels with a most ferocious tackle that flung the little Yale star back some twenty yards from the line of scrimmage. Albie got up in righteous indignation.

"Look here, Smith," he shrilled at the Georgia end, "there are a couple of things that absolutely do not go on this field, and roughness is one of them."

"Yeah," drawled Catfish Smith with a wide grin, "and you're the other."

☆ ☆ ☆

It doesn't happen very often, but this smart businessman let himself get into the clutches of a racetrack tout and proceeded to lose a great deal of money betting on the tips the fellow gave him. The tycoon took it as long as he could but then came to his senses and quit. The tout came looking for his soft touch on the last day of the race meeting. He found him in his office trying to earn back the money he had lost.

"What do you want?" demanded the businessman. "I told you I had enough of your lousy tips on horses."

"Don't be like that," said the tout. "I came here to give you a horse that will positively get you back on your feet."

"Get out of here!" screamed the businessman.

"Look, pal," said the tout. "I only want to prove to you that I'm your friend and want to help you. You can have this horse for free. I'll give you the name, and you can make a mental bet on him."

"A mental bet?" screeched the businessman. "Out, loafer! First you make me lose all my money, now you want I should lose my mind!"

☆ ☆ ☆

A silly story about a small boy who helped Papa to stay out of trouble deals with the time a fellow who loved to play the horses took his small son to watch the trotters and pacers. Papa brought the boy to the track early, then left him for a minute to see about getting a tip on the first race. When he came back, Sonny was watching one of the trotters who was warming up on the track in front of the stands.

"I'm going to bet on that one," said Papa. "I just got a big tip on him."

"Don't do it, Daddy," said the little boy.

"Why not?" asked Papa with a chuckle.

"He can't win," said the little boy.

"Are you sure?" asked the man.

"Positive," said the boy. "Better find another one to bet on, because this one lost his gasoline while you were away."

When Nat Holman was coaching the City College basketball teams that won so many championship honors over the years, the famous old-time player was noted for the care with which he expressed himself, particularly his diction and accent. Nevertheless, Nat, a New Yorker born

50

and bred, had been known to slip occasionally. During a practice session one day, Nat found it necessary to give a little advice to his players.

"Remember, boys," he said, "don't try to pa-a-ss (with broad 'a') until a-a-fter (with broad 'a') you see you won't be off (ah-f)."

"Why, coach?" asked an eager beaver.

"Why?" snapped Holman. "Because it's *moider* if you miss!"

Before he became President of the United States, Abraham Lincoln was quite an athlete. He was considered a great handball player, and recognized as a noted wrestler. Lincoln also fancied himself a good judge of horseflesh. He was sitting around with some old cronies one day when the subject of horses came up. The owner of several good race horses spoke up and ridiculed Lincoln's judgment of horseflesh.

"Tell you what," said Honest Abe to the owner of the race horses who had a reputation as a shrewd trader, "I'll make a horse trade with you, sight unseen. We'll each of us go out and bring back a horse and then we'll swap them. Whichever of us will want to back out, he will pay the other a forfeit of twenty-five dollars."

When word of the odd trade got around, a big crowd collected to await the return of the two men. When the owner of the several race horses returned, a howl of laughter went up at the sight of the skinny, sway-backed and ugly-looking animal he was leading on the end of a frayed bit of rope. But the laughter was nothing compared to the tremendous uproar that greeted the appearance of Lincoln, a few moments later. For Honest Abe was carrying a carpenter's sawhorse over his shoulder.

Abe Lincoln looked at the miserable spavined beast brought in by his rival. "Well, sir," he chuckled, "reckon you're too shrewd a horse trader for me because this is the first time I've been outwitted in a horse trade."

☆ ☆ ☆

This Kentucky breeder was trying to sell a hillbilly a horse. "Is he fast?" asked the hillbilly.

"Fast?" said the breeder. "He can go like the wind. Why, you could get on him tonight and be in Louisville by four o'clock in the morning."

"Four o'clock?" exclaimed the hillbilly. "What could I do so early in a big city?"

☆ ☆ ☆

St. Paul and St. Peter leaned over to watch a couple of duffers playing golf down below and decided to make a trip to earth to try the game themselves. St. Peter teed up first, measured the distance to the green with his eye, and drove the ball two hundred yards on a straight line. The ball hit the fairway, rolled up the green, and plopped into the cup. St. Paul smiled gently, teed up in turn, and smote the ball a real good belt. The little white pill sailed high and far, bounced once, and then cuddled cozily in the cup for another hole-in-one.

St. Peter shook his head and growled at St. Paul. "Come on," he said, "let's cut out the miracles and play some golf."

☆ ☆ ☆

If you want to make a football coach who has just finished a horrible and losing season laugh through his tears, tell him this classic that is heard across the land every year.

The head football coach was returning from the big game of the year (lost, needless to say) and, unable to sleep for worrying about his future, went wandering through the train. He got into a car that had been reserved for mental patients just as the man in white was checking up on his charges.

"One, two, three, four, five," the man counted, and then he spotted the unfamiliar face of the coach. "Who're you?"

"I'm a football coach," he answered with pride.

The male nurse nodded his head with understanding. ". . . six, seven, eight, nine . . ."

☆ ☆ ☆

A bookie was picked up in a raid and thrown into the clink. After a while he went nuts and was transferred to a lunatic asylum. Since none of the inmates had any money, they used pebbles to back their choices and the bookie did fine. In no time at all, he had all the pebbles in the place.

Then, one day, one of the fellows staggered up to the bookie with a big boulder on his shoulder. "Nothin' doin'!" screamed the daft bookie as he refused the bet. "With that big rock—you must know something!"

☆ ☆ ☆

One of Yale's immortals is Larry Kelley, All-American end of the 30's, a clever, cocky, pass-snaring wonder who was as quick with a quip as he was with an interception. The light-hearted Larry was as talkative as they come, but he was unusually silent one day during the opening minutes of a game against the bruising behemoths of the University of Pennsylvania. One of the Red and Blue's big linemen who had heard a great deal about Kelley's line of chatter could hold himself in no longer.

As Kelley climbed to his feet after a rough scrimmage, the big Penn lineman said, "I thought you were supposed to be the gabby type, Kelley. Cat got your tongue today?"

Kelley stared down his nose at the Penn man with an air of great surprise. "Oh, I didn't know," he exclaimed. "Do you guys speak English?"

☆ ☆ ☆

The Yale-Princeton game of 1934 resulted in a thrilling 7-0 victory for the Elis, the only touchdown of the game coming on a pass that Kelley caught and carried over the goal line. A few days later, Ducky Pond, Yale coach, called the squad together to watch the movies of the contest. Pond ran one section of the film through in slow motion in order to show the action of one of the backs during the play that ended in the winning pass. Then he ran the same portion of film through again so that he could criticize. Not entirely satisfied, he did this three or four times. Finally Kelley, a bored and sleepy expression on his face, interrupted the flow of words.

"Have a heart, coach," he yawned. "How about letting somebody else carry the ball?"

☆ ☆ ☆

The height of humiliation had been reached by a battered and beaten team of a certain Southern university. The point had arrived where all that was left to salvage was health and a whole skin. With a few minutes left to play, and trailing by six touchdowns, the quarterback got his boys together in a huddle.

"Number 36-A," he snapped. "Fullback through guard."

"Please!" gasped the fullback. "I couldn't run another step. They nearly broke my leg on that last time."

"Okay," chirped the quarterback, "make it 24-C, right half off left tackle."

"No!" groaned the right halfback. "You saw what happened when I tried that before. I lost three teeth!"

The quarterback let out a moan of despair. "All right, then," he said, "make it 24-F. Left half on buck lateral to the right."

"Don't you dare!" howled the left halfback. "Last time we tried that, I like to got killed!"

At this point the referee paced off five yards against the team for too much time in the huddle. Again the quarterback called his battered team together.

"Well?" he asked. "Any of you guys got any ideas what we ought to do?"

"Tell you what," piped up a guard brightly, "how about a nice long incomplete forward pass?"

☆ ☆ ☆

A fellow had been out on the links practicing and came back to the locker room looking pale and badly shaken.

"What's wrong?" asked his friend.

"I just killed my mother-in-law!" groaned the unhappy man.

"Holy mackerel!" exclaimed the friend. "How in the world did you do that?"

"I was out there practicing," said the man. "I didn't see her come up behind me. I took a back swing. It hit her on the head and she dropped right in her tracks—dead."

"Terrible," murmured the friend. "What club were you using?"

"A number two iron," moaned the man.

"Aha!" said his friend happily. *"That's* the club!"

☆ ☆ ☆

Buddy Baer is the big, lumbering kid brother of the former heavyweight champion, Max Baer. Buddy came within a single punch of becoming world's champion himself, but is best known today as a movie actor and stage performer with a surprising amount of polish for a man his size. Buddy proved his newly acquired presence of mind on the stage one day when a heckler flung a question at him right in the middle of his performance.

"Hey, Buddy," the heckler yelled from the audience, "what about taxes?"

"I love Texas," replied Buddy. "Greatest state in the union!"

"No, no," shouted the heckler. "I mean dollars!"

"Oh, Dallas," said Buddy Baer. "Why, Dallas is one of the finest cities in Texas!"

☆ ☆ ☆

Casey Stengel was managing the Boston Braves and Tommy Holmes, a young rookie at the time, took his place at the plate for batting practice. After a minute or two, Casey stepped forward.

"Look, kid," he said, "you don't seem able to pull the ball down that first-base line. Now you watch me do it. I used to be an expert at pulling the ball."

Casey grabbed Holmes's bat and called for a pitch. The hurler reared back and let fly a high sailer that conked poor Casey right on top of the head. The Boston manager bit the dust, his legs kicking. Then he slowly dragged himself to his feet and turned to Holmes.

"I guess we better demonstrate what I was telling you tomorrow," groaned Casey. "That big lug in the box just put me on base."

☆ ☆ ☆

George Fisher, once a major-league outfielder, without doubt had the worst day a ballplayer ever had.

One afternoon while playing for Minneapolis, he came to bat five times—and five times he struck out. Added to his misery, he dropped a fly ball, which cost his team the game. To add to his woes for that one afternoon, the only ball he managed to touch when at bat was a line drive foul which he poked over the wall. The ball bounced into the street outside the ballpark. When the game was over, the irate manager of the Minneapolis team, Mike Kelly, rushed up to Fisher and screamed:

"It ain't bad enough you didn't get a hit—it ain't bad enough you struck out five times—and I can even stand your lousing up that fly ball that lost us the game—but that foul ball you hit out of the ballpark broke a plate glass window in a store across the street and the owner just handed me a bill for five hundred bucks. You're going to pay it out of your salary—you no-good bum."

☆ ☆ ☆

When the late Joe Cantillon was managing at Minneapolis, he had as one of his pitchers a fellow named Harry Harper who was so wild he almost drove his manager crazy. Harper had been known to issue as many as twenty bases on balls in a game. One very windy day, Cantillon sent Harper to the mound in desperation, and the wild man began to hand out the walks. After a couple of innings, Harper started looking towards the bench in the hope that Cantillon would take pity on him and lift him for another pitcher.

Cantillon squirmed on the bench until he could contain himself no longer. "I'm not going to take you out," he yelled at the harassed pitcher. "Stay out there and throw. First thing you know, the wind's going to blow a strike over the plate for you!"

☆ ☆ ☆

A Russian wolfhound paid a visit to one of his distant relatives, an English racing greyhound. "How are things here in London, comrade?" asked the Russian wolfhound.

"Not too good," replied the greyhound. "Food is kind of scarce these days. And how is it in Moscow?"

"Food we got," answered the wolfhound. "Plenty meat, plenty bones, lots food, everything is fine. Shortages, we don't got at all."

"Still you come to England to live," said the greyhound. "Why, if things are so good over there?"

"Well," muttered the wolfhound, "I'll tell you. A fellow likes to bark once in a while, too."

☆ ☆ ☆

Nick Lukats, one of Notre Dame's former gridiron greats, was visiting with some old friends he had not seen for a long time. The friends wondered about whether the old campus had changed much and kept pouring questions about the old and familiar landmarks so dear to them.

At the entrance to the campus in South Bend there is a statue of Father Sorin, the priest who founded Notre Dame. The statue stands on a pedestal and has been there for many years. It shows the good father with his right arm extended straight up to heaven.

"How about the statue of Father Sorin?" one of his friends asked Nick Lukats. "Is it still where it used to be?"

"Oh, yes," replied Lukats with a smile.

"Then tell me," the friend continued, "is he still signaling for a fair catch?"

☆ ☆ ☆

Foreign-made cars have caught the fancy of the American public, and the low-slung, Continental racer is very much in demand these days. Second-hand dealers are never at a loss for words, of course, and one of them was handing a hot prospect a real line about a Jaguar car he was trying to sell him.

"This beautiful car," he said, "used to belong to my aunt, now dead, poor thing. Only used it to drive to church every Sunday. Took the best care of it."

"Only used it to go to church?" asked the prospect. "Why would she need a car that makes over a hundred miles an hour just to drive to church?"

"Oh," answered the second-hand dealer, "my aunt was so religious, she just couldn't wait to get there!"

☆ ☆ ☆

Cardinal Spellman once accepted a friend's invitation to see a charity boxing match. As the fight was about to begin, one of the fighters genuflected in his corner and crossed himself.

"Is that going to do him any good?" whispered the friend to His Eminence.

The Cardinal hesitated a moment before replying. "Of course it will," he said at last. "Provided he can punch."

☆ ☆ ☆

The Centre College team had somehow acquired the nickname of "Praying Colonels" on the report that Charley Moran led his players in prayer before each game.

Moran brought his little team to Cambridge one year to upset Harvard in the most startling form reversal on the gridiron. A few minutes before Centre was to take the field, the players were chatting and laughing in the locker room, waiting to go out.

Suddenly the door burst open and Moran flung himself into the room. "Down on your knees, quick!" he gasped. "A reporter's coming!"

☆ ☆ ☆

A boy who was fascinated by a demonstration of boomerang-hurling finally succeeded in talking his father into getting him one. The boy practiced faithfully with his boomerang until he became as expert with it as an Australian bushman. Then, when his birthday came along, all he wanted as a present from his father was a new boomerang.

A few weeks later, a friend of the family heard that the boy had been placed in an institution. He called the father on the telephone. "What happened?" he asked.

The father groaned. "You remember I got him a new boomerang for his birthday?" he sighed. "Well, he went out of his mind trying to throw the old one away."

A couple of horse players who went to the track every day fell into conversation on the train going home. "I can't do a thing right," one wailed. "I haven't had a winner in weeks. And you?"

"I'm doing fine," said the other. "Got me a little system that's been working like a charm. All I do is stop in at the church for ten or fifteen minutes every morning on the way to the track and pray."

The heavy loser pondered a while. "I'll try that myself," he said finally. "Thanks."

A few days later the two met again. "I did as you said," the man who had been losing complained. "It hasn't done me a bit of good. I still haven't had a winner."

"I can't understand it," said the other. "Did you really pray?"

"I certainly did," said the loser. "As hard as I could."

"Where did you go?" asked the man who had been winning.

"St. Bernard's," said the unlucky one.

"St. Bernard's? No wonder you can't win!" cried the other.

"What's the matter with St. Bernard's?" demanded the big loser.

"Oh, nothing, nothing!" replied the winner hastily. "Only thing is, *that* church is strictly for *trotters!*"

☆ ☆ ☆

The laziest ballplayer ever to pull on a pair of cleated shoes was a semi-pro pitcher who performed for a sandlot outfit somewhere in West Texas. He did everything in a slow and vague manner. Everything, that is, except pitch. Aside from that, the kid was bone-lazy.

One hot Sabbath afternoon, the lazy youngster's team was in a tight contest with another outfit from a neighboring town. Midway in the game, the lazy kid was suddenly ordered into the contest as a relief pitcher. He pulled himself together and shuffled slowly to the dusty mound.

The umpire, who had been handling the game from behind the mound because he had neither mask nor chest protector, waited patiently for young lazy-bones. The hurler made a few slow-motion warm-up tosses to the plate. At no time did he stop to look around him. Finally he took a deep breath and spoke for the first time.

"How many on base?" he drawled.

The umpire's mouth popped open with astonishment. "Just one," he finally said. "There's a runner on second."

Young lazy-bones started a long slow stretch. When his arms were out in front of him as far as they would go, he spoke again.

"How big's his lead?" he asked.

59

The game between Notre Dame and Southern Methodist had scarcely begun when the Fighting Irish scored a touchdown. A spectator sprang to his feet, let out a screech of delight and pounded his neighbor on the back.

A few minutes later, SMU scored and the same spectator went through the same routine. The neighbor's curiosity was aroused. "Who are you rooting for, friend?" he asked.

"I don't care who wins," replied the spectator. "I just came out to enjoy the game."

"Aha," sneered the neighbor, "an atheist."

☆ ☆ ☆

Father Bill Daly is one of the legendary characters of the racing world. Much of his fame rested on his ability to make great jockeys out of green kids and winning horses out of patched up cripples. Many a long shot came home winning with old Bill's money riding on his nose.

Father Bill had a lot of his own tricks for getting an old cripple ready for a race. One day an official of the Society for the Prevention of Cruelty to Animals came around to the barn to see what the veteran trainer might be up to. As luck would have it, Father Bill had an ancient gelding standing in a steaming tub of boiling hot water.

"Here, you can't do that," protested the SPCA official. "It's downright cruel to make a horse stand in boiling water."

"The water isn't that hot," replied Father Bill. "I'll prove it to you." And he stuck his own leg into the tub to show that it was quite comfortable.

Satisfied, the SPCA official went on his way. As soon as he was out of sight, Father Bill lifted his leg from the tub, rolled up his trouser and carefully wiped off—his *wooden leg*.

☆ ☆ ☆

Lou Little, former Columbia football coach, was blessed with a wonderful sense of humor, a quality that stood him in good stead over his years.

It was during one game that Lou was suddenly startled to discover that he had twelve men on the field. The opposition ran several plays and still the officials did not notice the error. At last Lou was able to send in a new quarterback with instructions to send the other signal caller and another player to the bench.

When the two men came running to the sideline, Lou called the young quarterback over. "Tell me," he began, "Why did you use that 6-2-2-2 defense out there? Why didn't you try 7-2-2-1 instead?"

The youngster looked puzzled. "Why, coach," he replied, "how could I? You haven't even taught us that one yet!"

☆ ☆ ☆

Another time it was a Columbia sophomore tackle who got into trouble on the field. He complained to the referee that he was being held.

"Go on back there and play," said the official. "I'll watch and see what's happening to you."

A few plays later, the official called the tackle to one side. "Nobody's holding you, son," he said. "You're being mousetrapped."

"Mousetrapped?" exclaimed the youngster. "What's that?"

The referee hurriedly explained.

"Gosh," said the youngster. "You mean to say they let me go through on purpose?"

"That's right," said the official.

"Well, I'll be durned," said the sophomore tackle. "That's a wonderful trick. I'm going to tell Mr. Little all about it!"

☆ ☆ ☆

Here's a sad story that proves you can't beat the horses. This fellow went to the races one day. In the first race, his eye was caught by the name, Charley Boy. Since his own name was Charley, he looked further. Charley Boy's number was three. Today was the third birthday of Charley's twins. Charley Boy's colors were blue and pink. Charley's twins were a boy and a girl. How could it miss? It all added up. So Charley went and put his all on Charley Boy.

Unfortunately, Charley Boy came in a dead last. "That'll teach me," mourned Charley. "I'll never make another bet on a sure thing."

☆ ☆ ☆

Lou Kusserow, one of Lou Little's greatest backs, made the Columbia team as a freshman, along with Gene Rossides. Before his first game, Lou Little warned Kusserow not to try to run back kick-offs if they went over the goal line, but to down the ball in the end zone.

The opening kick-off went to Kusserow over the goal line. Lou fumbled, recovered, fumbled again, grabbed the ball and started to run.

On the bench, Little sprang to his feet, his face red with anger. "Get that fool kid out of there!'' he yelled to his assistant. Kusserow had reached his own ten-yard line and seemed trapped by a host of tacklers. Somehow, he squirmed away and wasn't caught until he had reached the enemy eight-yard line.

Little stuck out a hand to stop his assistant from carrying out the instruction he had just given.

"Let the kid stay in," Lou Little growled. "After all, he's only seventeen years old. You wouldn't want to shake his self-confidence, would you?"

A team of Ants was playing football against a team of Elephants. One of the Ant backs tried to go past an Elephant end with the ball and was crushed to death when the pachyderm stuck out a foot.

The crowd let out a howl of indignation and the referee blew his whistle and called time. Then he bawled out the offending player.

"What's the idea?" he yelled. "Why did you step on that poor little Ant and kill him?"

The big Elephant hung his head. "Aw, gee," he said, "I was only trying to trip him up."

☆ ☆ ☆

A couple of fishermen got into a rowboat at a New Orleans dock. Johnny said suddenly that he felt like rowing all the way to Chicago.

"Why, stupid," said the other, "that's impossible!"

"It is not impossible," answered Johnny stoutly. "If I row all night I'm sure I can make Chicago by tomorrow morning."

As Johnny got ready to row, his friend stepped out of the rowboat and tied it to the dock. Johnny then began to row. He rowed and rowed right through the night. In the morning, his wife came down to the dock.

"Johnny!" she called. "What are you doing, Johnny?"

Johnny shipped his oars and looked up. "Why, Daisy!" he cried. "How did you get to Chicago before I did?"

☆ ☆ ☆

The next day Johnny and his pal went fishing in the Gulf. The fish were plentiful and in no time they had a boat load. Came the next morning, and the two men went fishing again. This time they caught nothing at all.

"Say, Johnny," asked the friend, "are you sure we're in the same spot we came to yesterday?"

"I certainly am," answered Johnny. "I even marked the place."

"You did?" said the friend, looking around. "I don't see anything in the water."

"Oh, I didn't mark the water," said Johnny. "See over here"—and he pointed out a big X—"I marked the side of the boat!"

☆ ☆ ☆

Don Budge was playing a tennis exhibition in Kansas with Frank Kovacs. Kovacs, a clown of the court, played in cowboy boots, chaps, spurs and ten-gallon Stetson. The audience fell into the mood, shouting "Yippee!" at every shot and showering the court with small coins. Kovacs picked up the coins on his side of the court and stuck them into his pocket.

Budge was annoyed with the antics of the crowd and his opponent. He finally came to the net and called across to Kovacs. "Hey," he asked, "you got any more good ideas?"

"Yeah," replied Kovacs as he eyed the coins scattered on Budge's side of the net, "let's change courts."

☆ ☆ ☆

A murderer, condemned to be hanged, was visited by the warden the night before the execution.

"Is there anything you'd like to do before we—er—spring the trap?" asked the warden.

"Yes, I would," replied the murderer who happened to be a golf nut. "I'd like to try a practice swing."

Out on the golf course things were pretty even for the first few holes. After the fourth hole, one of the golfers turned to his friend who was marking his card.

"How many did you take on that one?" he asked.

"Nine," replied his friend.

"That was my hole, then," said the first golfer. "I only took eight."

After the next hole had been played, the first player asked his friend the same question.

"Oh, no," said the other bitterly, "it's my turn to ask first this time!"

This fellow and his dog came into the tavern and sat down at the bar.

"Nice dog," said the bartender.

"Not only that," said the fellow. "He talks."

"That I don't believe," said the bartender.

"I'll show you," said the fellow. "What's on top of a house?"

"R-r-roof!" answered the dog promptly.

"Good dog," said the fellow. "And how's business these days?"

"R-r-rough!" exclaimed the dog.

"Too bad," said the fellow. "Now tell us, who was the longest hitter in baseball?"

"R-r-ru-uth!" growled the dog.

"Nuts!" snorted the bartender. "What a fake!" And he threw the fellow and his dog out of the tavern.

"Shame on you," said the fellow sadly as he picked himself up off the sidewalk.

"Yeah," mumbled the dog apologetically. "Maybe I should have said Mickey Mantle?"

☆ ☆ ☆

It was back in 1916 that Georgia Tech ran up the record score for a football game when they crushed little Cumberland College of Lebanon, Tenn., 222 to 0.

Cumberland was taking a terrific beating. Tech, fired up by the mounting score, was hitting so hard and tackling so viciously that the bewildered and disheartened Cumberland players were merely going through the motions of playing football. Then Cumberland took the ball after a Tech kick-off. On the first play, a battered and weary Cumberland back fumbled. The ball bounced crazily and came to rest at the feet of a fresh substitute who had just been sent into the game. The fumbling back let out a shout, "Fall on it, Bill!"

The substitute took one quick look at the big Georgia Tech lineman bearing down on him. "Fall on it yourself!" he yelped. "It's *your* fumble!" And he hastily retreated to safety behind his own goal line.

☆ ☆ ☆

As the third quarter drew to a close, one of the Cumberland players, his eyes glazed with fatigue, was replaced and sent out of the game. He staggered uncertainly, then turned and tottered towards the Georgia Tech sideline. When he collapsed on the bench, the Tech coach came over to him.

"Say, son," asked the coach kindly, "are you all right?"

"I'm fine," mumbled the battered player.

"You're on the wrong bench," said the coach gently.

"Oh, no, I'm not," said the player. "This is the Georgia Tech side, isn't it?"

"Yes."

"Well, then," said the player with satisfaction, "this is the only place I'm safe. If I go back to my bench, I'm liable to get sent back in the game again!"

☆ ☆ ☆

Before Joe Louis became heavyweight champion, he was sent out on tour across the country meeting a lot of willing but unskillful opponents at the rate of one a week. One of these boxers came to town for his match and was led by his manager to a backstreet hotel before the fight. When they got to their room, the fighter undressed and got into bed.

"I hear this guy Louis is pretty good," he mumbled. "I better get some rest before taking him on."

That evening, he climbed into the ring, touched gloves with the Brown Bomber, and then took a vicious right that sent him to dreamland. After the referee had finished the count, the victim's manager got him dressed and took him back to the hotel.

When they got to the room, the addled boxer began to take off his tie and shirt.

"Whatcha doin'?" asked his manager.

"I hear this guy Louis is pretty good," said the boxer. "If I'm going to take him on tonight, I'd better get some rest!"

☆ ☆ ☆

Baseball has always had its share of eccentric characters, but none will be remembered longer or more fondly than Babe Herman, one-time hero of the daffy Brooklyn Dodgers.

It was a hot summer's day. Babe appeared in his hotel lobby elegantly attired in a suit of purest white silk. A young lady smiled at the great hero.

"My," she said, "how cool you look."

Babe blushed with embarrassment, then glanced at the sleeveless low-necked dress the young lady had on. "Thank you, miss," he gulped. "You don't look so hot yourself."

☆ ☆ ☆

This happened to Lone Star Dietz who coached the Boston Redskin football professionals some years ago. Lone Star preferred to do his coaching during games from the pressbox where he could get a better view of the proceedings on the gridiron below.

Before the kick-off (the Redskins were playing the New York Giants at Fenway Park), Lone Star called his boys together. "If you win the toss," he said, "I want you to elect to kick off to the Giants. Got that?"

The boys nodded and Lone Star took off on the long long climb up the Fenway Park ramp to the pressbox. He finally reached it and came through the door. To his great astonishment, he saw the Redskins lining up to receive the kick-off.

Lone Star grabbed the phone and started cussing out the Boston bench. "I thought I told you to kick off!" he roared.

"We did kick off, coach," was the answer. "Where've you been? The score is now 7-0."

☆ ☆ ☆

Brooklyn once owned a pitcher named Walter Beck who was a very nice guy but whose pitching left much to be desired. So often were his best deliveries slammed against the fences that he acquired the unenviable nickname of "Boom-Boom" from the sound that filled the ball park by opposing batters.

The late Hack Wilson, short pudgy outfielder and home-run hitter, was patrolling right field in Brooklyn one day when Boom-Boom was on the mound, and the hits were flying around his ears. Hack chased them this way and that way, up and down the field, until he was exhausted. At last, Manager Casey Stengel came out to the mound to derrick Boom-Boom. Hack, out in right field, sagged with relief, his eyes cast down.

Beck, however, did not want to leave the game. He argued bitterly with Stengel; then, seeing it was no use, he spun on his heel and fired the ball at the right-field fence. Hack did not see him do it. Startled out of his reverie, he wheeled quickly as the ball ricocheted off the fence. He chased it down, grabbed it and threw with the same motion—a perfect peg to second base to hold the nonexistent runner to a double off the fence!

☆ ☆ ☆

Boom-Boom Beck's reputation for throwing line-drive hits against enemy bats got into strange places, as is indicated by the following story.

Several of the Brooklyn players were invited to visit a hospital to talk baseball with the patients. Boom-Boom accepted gladly and, accompanied by a doctor, came into one of the wards where he was immediately surrounded by eager faces. He began to talk about pitching, when he was interrupted by one of the patients.

"Yah, go on, ya bum," jeered the patient. "You're the guy who's always getting knocked out of the box!"

Boom-Boom left the ward in confusion. On the way out, the doctor started to apologize. "I'm sorry," he said, "I should have told you that was the psychopathic ward." And then, as if it were an afterthought, he added, "Say, you know what? That was the first sane remark that fellow's made since he came in here!"

☆ ☆ ☆

A fellow swears he saw this happen one day at one of those half-mile tracks where lots of odd things are known to happen. A race horse stepped out of the parade to the post and ambled up to the two-dollar window.

"Give me a two-buck win ticket on myself," said the horse. The startled mutuel clerk let out a howl of laughter.

"What's the matter?" asked the horse. "You laughing at me because I can talk?"

"Naw," said the clerk. "I'm laughing at you because you think you can win!"

☆ ☆ ☆

One afternoon, enemy bats were shelling "Boom-Boom" Beck heavier than usual. He raged into his dugout and violently kicked the water bucket.

"Here, here, cut that out!" manager Stengel gently admonished him. "If you break your leg, I can't trade you!"

During the winter lay-off from racing, a fellow who owned some trotting horses was breezing one of his charges down a back road in the country one day. He stopped before a little tavern and stepped inside.

"What's yours?" asked the bartender politely.

"I'd like a double bourbon and a bucket," said the horseman. The bartender obliged, and the owner poured the bourbon into the bucket, added just a little water, then took it outside and served it to the shivering horse.

"That was a real nice thing to do," said the bartender when the man returned the empty bucket. "And I'd like to offer you a drink on the house. What'll it be?"

"Sorry, not for me," said the horse owner sadly. "I'm driving."

This fellow was advised by his doctor to try horseback riding in order to lose some weight. Never having been on a horse in his life, Chubby approached the animal with a great deal of caution. The horse, aware that his rider was a greenhorn, got pretty nervous and began to jiggle around a little. Fatso got more nervous than ever and the horse took to bucking. Finally the horse caught its rear hoof in a stirrup. The man on his back looked down in amazement.

"Look here, horse," he said, "I don't like this. If you're going to get on, by golly, then I'm going to get off!"

☆ ☆ ☆

A stranger accosted John McGraw one afternoon while on the way to the ball park. "What do you want?" barked the little Napoleon.

"How about a pass for today's game?" asked the stranger.

"Why should I give you a pass?" asked McGraw.

"I'm a friend of the umpire, Bill Klem," answered the other.

"No pass!" snapped the little Giant manager.

"Why not?" asked the stranger.

"Because you're a liar!" shouted McGraw. "No umpire ever had a friend!"

☆ ☆ ☆

Boxing referees have had many odd situations to meet as part of their job. None was more unusual than that faced by Young Otto.

Young Otto had been a great lightweight fighter in his day. When his fighting days were over, Otto became a fine referee. One night he was assigned to handle an entire card of fights. After he had refereed all the preliminaries with his usual skill, Young Otto was informed that the main event could not go on because one of the opponents had failed to show up. The crowd, bitterly disappointed, began to boo and protest.

Otto raised his hands for silence. "A little patience," he announced. "I'll get you a worthy substitute for the missing man."

He left the ring and reappeared a few minutes later in trunks, ready to fight. The rugged middleweight who was waiting in the other corner laughed. "You're not going to fight me, are you, pop?" he jeered. "You're too old and you're liable to get hurt. And who's going to referee? We can't fight without a third man in the ring!"

"You just come out fighting at the bell," answered Young Otto. "I'm still the referee, and when I knock you out, I'll do the counting myself."

And, oddly enough, referee Young Otto did flatten his opponent in four rounds. Then he counted his victim out, and to prove the fight was on the level, he repeated the count of ten over his fallen and unconscious opponent!

☆ ☆ ☆

Years ago, when Ban Johnson, president of the American League, and the first Czar of Baseball, canvassed all the big-league umpires for suggestions on how to keep baseball games from consuming too much time, it was tough Tim Hurst who put an end to all that nonsense. His simple answer was: "Cut them to six innings."

☆ ☆ ☆

There may never again be a big-league umpire as colorful as the late George Magerkurth. A one-time prizefighter, Magerkurth was one umpire who relished a fight. He is credited with being the only umpire in major-league history who, when hit by a pop bottle thrown by an irate fan, picked it up and threw it back into the stands, hitting the original throw-

70

er with it. He was the only umpire who ever got the upper hand in the matter of conversation with Leo "The Lip" Durocher, the most tempestuous umpire baiter of modern times.

Big Mage was umpiring at first one day when Lippy Durocher was coaching there. That noted umpire fighter was in rare conversational form. But after five or six innings, Lippy's yakking got on the arbiter's nerves.

"For goshsakes, Leo, shut up!" roared Magerkurth. "One more word out of you, and you're out of the game!"

The threat zipped up The Lip. For it was an important game, and Durocher wanted to stick around. But an inning later, one of Durocher's players was called out at first on a hair-line play. The Lip couldn't take a chance on a vocal protest, so instead he simulated a faint, keeling over backwards, to fall flat on the ground. Umpire Magerkurth bridled at the travesty. He studied the fallen manager for a minute, and then he roared:

"The runner is still out. And you, Durocher, dead or alive, you're out of the game, too."

☆ ☆ ☆

The famous football referee Tiny Maxwell used to chuckle about this one dealing with penalties. He was officiating in a game which saw one of the teams having a terrible time staying within the rules. They would make a big gain through the line, and Tiny would slap a five-yard penalty on them for backfield illegally in motion. Another big gain would draw a fifteen-yard penalty for offensive holding. Finally, the harassed team pulled a spectacular forward pass that brought the ball to the opponent's one-yard line, just as the first quarter ended.

Tiny picked up the ball and started up the field for the change of goals. As he passed midfield, the captain of the team in possession could not hold himself in any longer.

"Have a heart!" he screamed at Maxwell. "You're handing us the most unfair penalty I ever saw!"

☆ ☆ ☆

Of all the incidents in which big Mage was involved, none is more amusing and memorable than the one that involved the little ex-con who came out of the stands one day to do him battle for the honor of the Brooklyn Dodgers.

A play had taken place at second base which resulted in one of those typical rhubarbs to which Dodger fans have long since become accustomed. Magerkurth saw fit to change another umpire's decision. The decision was against Brooklyn and the stands went wild with rage. Suddenly a squat little figure emerged from the grandstand and descended on big Magerkurth. A moment later, Mage was rolling ignominiously in the dust with the little guy astride him and pummeling him for all he was worth. Police swarmed on the field. The little guy was hauled away.

In police court it was discovered that the little guy was out on parole. He was quickly slapped back into the pen, even though Magerkurth refused to press assault charges against the little guy. They asked big Mage why he was so willing to let bygones be bygones.

"Aw, shucks," Magerkurth said with magnificent aplomb, "I got a boy of my own."

☆ ☆ ☆

They tell a silly story about a not-too-bright umpire who was working a game on a dark and dismal day. It got darker and darker as the game progressed until it was almost impossible to see anything that was happening on the field. It was then that the pitcher for one of the teams got a bright idea. As the batter took his stance at the plate, the pitcher wound up and threw as hard as he could towards the plate. That is, he acted as if he threw. In fact, he did not let go of the ball.

The batter, thinking he saw the blur of the ball as it came up to the plate, swung. "Strike one!" yelled the umpire.

The catcher made believe he was throwing the ball back to the mound. The pitcher pretended to catch it, rubbed it up a little, and again faked making the pitch. Again the batter swung and missed. "Strike two!" barked the umpire.

The battery mates went through the same routine again. Again the pitcher pretended to throw the ball to the plate. This time the batter, figuring that the man on the mound was going to waste one, refused to offer at the imaginary pitch. To his amazement, the umpire yelled out, "Strike three! You're out!"

The batter turned furiously on the umpire. "You're crazy, man!" he screamed. "Anybody could see that wasn't a strike!"

"What do you mean, it wasn't a strike?" quoth the umpire.

"See for yourself," snarled the batter as he rolled up his sleeve. "It hit me right here on the arm!"

☆　☆　☆

A legendary figure in the world of boxing is the late James Joy Johnston, little English-born manager of hallowed memory. In the old days when boxing was more of a sport than it is today, Johnston, sometimes known as "The Boy Bandit," handled the affairs of the great Ted Kid Lewis. According to the records, Lewis met the welterweight champion, Jack Britton, twenty-two times in the ring. This story deals with the first meeting between the two men. It may not have been as bloody an encounter as subsequent ones, but it was by far the funniest.

The men were matched to go fifteen rounds to a decision in the fair city of Boston. On the day of the contest, Britton showed up not only with his manager, Dumb Dan Morgan, but also with a hand-picked referee.

When Jimmy Johnston learned about this, he held his counsel until the referee entered the ring with the two fighters. Then he edged over to the row of reporters at ringside.

"Gentlemen," he shouted at the top of his voice, "I want you to know that Britton's got his own referee in there. This fight is not going to be decided on its merits!"

The referee, who had heard Johnston's remarks all too clearly in the center of the ring, glowered through the ropes at the little man from Liverpool.

"What's more," continued Johnston loudly, "I'm sure this guy's going to rob me!"

"Shut up!" shouted the red-faced referee. "You'll get a square deal and you know it!"

"Says you," jeered Johnston. "This isn't the first time I've run into your kind. It's an insult to the fine fans of Boston to bring in an outsider as referee."

"Shut that guy up!" yelled Morgan suddenly from Britton's corner. "Shut him up or I'll come over and do it myself!"

Meanwhile, Britton, as incensed as his manager, started for Lewis. The two men began to mix it up in a corner and seconds, handlers, and everyone else who could get into the ring pitched in with a will. The police poured into the ring after a few minutes and stopped the general melee. At last, all was cleared and the real fight could begin.

The bell rang for the first round. The two boys sparred in the center of the ring. There was a commotion in Lewis' corner. Then Jimmy Johnston stuck his head up and shook his fist at the referee. "Robber!" he screamed. "Look at that guy robbing us! Oh, you crook!"

The referee turned his head in startled surprise. "You're getting a square deal, Johnston!" he shouted. "I'm as honest as you are, you loud-mouthed bandit!"

And so it went, all through the fight. With every exchange of punches in the ring, Johnston let out a roar of protest. To every insult the referee answered in self-defense. The ringside was in a constant uproar as the bewildered referee spent more time denying Johnston's charges than he did watching the fight he was supposed to judge.

At the end of the contest, there was a loud buzz of speculation from all sides. In his corner, Dumb Dan Morgan chuckled with satisfaction as he patted his boy Britton on the back. In the other corner, the downcast Jimmy Johnston growled and grumbled. In all that mass of people, only these two, the managers of Lewis and Britton, thought there was no question as to what the decision would be.

Britton had won by the proverbial mile. The bell clanged for silence. The referee hesitated for a moment. Then, as the crowd roared, he swiftly crossed the ring and lifted the hand of Ted Kid Lewis in token of victory. Jimmy Johnston's boy had won!

Dumb Dan Morgan nearly swooned. Jimmy Johnston was so shocked that he actually tumbled off the stool on which he was sitting. And then things began to pop. Again the enraged Jack Britton flung himself across the ring at Ted Kid Lewis. Again there was a wild battle that swept across the ring from one side to the other. Only one man held his position as the renewed war surged around him. Only one voice could be heard above the terrific racket. Jimmy Johnston clung to the ropes before the press row, a look of wounded dignity on his face. "Cut it out, fellows," he bellowed. "What are you all so excited about? The referee's an honest man, I tell you! There's no reason to squawk about the decision. He called it as he saw it! He's an honest man!"

☆ ☆ ☆

Max Baer was the only fighter in boxing history who clowned his way to the heavyweight championship of the world. Famed as "The Magnificent Screwball," his zest for wild living and his zany antics were legendary. Nevertheless, that playboy-champ was a fist fighter great enough to gain enshrinement in Boxing's Hall of Fame.

The shortest and most amusing interview champion Max Baer ever gave was the time when a youthful editor of a widely read schoolboy newspaper was ushered into the great man's presence. The world's heavyweight king held a drink in one hand, and a beautiful blond was on his knee.

"Mr. Baer, how did you become the heavyweight boxing champion of the world?" asked the eager youngster.

"By clean living, kid. Clean and wholesome living!" replied champion Max Baer.

☆ ☆ ☆

A famous billiard champion got disturbed when his game began to fall off. He found that whenever he bent over the table to make a shot his ears started ringing and he eyes popped out of his head. On the advice of friends, he went to see a specialist.

"I don't give you a year to live," said the doctor gravely. "Make the best of it."

"That I will," murmured the cue wizard, and proceeded to suit the action to the word. He bought a fancy convertible, 24 suits, 15 pairs of shoes, and then checked over the rest of his wardrobe. "I think I'd better get some new shirts," he decided. "And nothing but the best."

He hopped into his new car and drove to the fanciest shirt shop in town. "I want two dozen made-to-order shirts," he demanded.

"They'll be quite expensive," said the haughty clerk.

"What's money to me?" mourned the billiard champ. "Fix me up."

"All right," said the clerk, "let's take your measurements. Sleeve, 35. Collar, 16-1/2 . . ."

"You mean 15-1/2," interposed the doomed man.

75

"I mean 16-1/2," insisted the clerk.

"Wait a minute!" interrupted the billiard champ angrily. "I always wear a 15-1/2 shirt."

"Look, my good man," said the clerk loftily, "you can have your shirts made with a 15-1/2 collar, but if you do, you'll have a ringing in your ears and your eyes will pop out!"

Fabled Babe Ruth's greatest asset in life was an ability to laugh, and also make the baseball world laugh at his hilarious escapades. When the immortal Babe was in full flower as the greatest home-run hitter of all time, Marshall Foch, France's greatest general in the first World War, visited Yankee Stadium to see a baseball game for the first time. Babe Ruth was delegated to bid the war hero welcome.

When those two great men met, the Babe looked at Marshall Foch's handsome powder-blue uniform, and the many medals and decorations on his chest, forgot his welcome-speech, and blurted out:

"Hey, General! They tell me you were in the war!"

☆ ☆ ☆

At the end of the 1968 football season, after winning the championship of the American Football League, the players of the victorious New York Jets, with their happy wives, were given a party. Each married player, when called on to speak, glowingly thanked his wife for being a loyal and cooperative helpmate by showing unusual patience and understanding all through that glorious season. When it was the turn of the Jets' fabulous quarterback Joe Namath to speak, the team's most celebrated playboy-bachelor arose and simply said:

"And I want to thank all the broads in town."

☆ ☆ ☆

There have been many "holler guys" in collegiate basketball coaching, but the basketball coach who did more jumping off the bench and more shouting from the sidelines than any other college basketball coach was Lou Carnesecca of the 1968 powerful St. John's University team.

"Why do you waste all that energy?" he once was asked. "Your players on the court don't hear what you're yelling at them, anyway."

"Thank God!" said winning basketball coach Carnesecca.

☆ ☆ ☆

One year, when the Chicago White Sox finished the season deep in the second division, their manager Jack Onslow was a most unhappy fellow. The following year he decided that his players would prepare themselves much better for the new season if their wives stayed away from the White Sox training camp. Politely, he requested that they do so.

But one wife firmly disagreed. She was a chunky, aggressive wife of one of the outfielders. She not only accompanied her husband to camp, but attended all the exhibition games played by the White Sox, and often commented loudly on the management of the team.

"I'm here and you can't put me out!" she yelled one afternoon at manager Onslow from her seat in the stands. "Where my husband goes, I go!"

"Great!" shouted the exasperated White Sox manager from the third-base coaching box. "Madam, how would Beaumont in the Texas League suit you?" And that's where he shipped her outfielder-husband the following day.

☆ ☆ ☆

When home-run slugger Dick Stuart was playing in the major leagues, and wandering from club to club, he spread many managerial headaches because of his atrocious fielding as a first baseman.

One day, when Stuart was playing for Pittsburgh, the Pirates went into the bottom of the ninth with a one-run lead over St. Louis. With two out, a Cardinal hitter rapped a hot one to short, but the throw got to Dick Stuart at first 'way ahead of the runner. Zany Stuart tried to get away with a quick and dramatic tag of the base. His foot missed the bag entirely. The umpire called the runner safe.

Out of the Pirates' dugout and onto the field came manager Danny Murtaugh, blazing with fury.

"Now, now, Danny, control yourself," advised the first-base umpire soothingly. "I called that one right."

"Get out of my way," angrily barked manager Murtaugh. "I'm not after you this time. I'm after that lousy first baseman of mine."

☆ ☆ ☆

Few catchers in major-league history were the equal of Yogi Berra in backstop greatness. But no one was his equal in saying humorous things, unconsciously.

Once when asked how things were going for him, he nimbly replied: "I'm straddling the other side of the fence right now." Another time, when he was asked what he thought about Little League baseball, he seriously replied: "I think it's good, because it keeps the kids out of the house."

☆ ☆ ☆

When Ralph Kiner, one-time home-run king of the major leagues, married the one-time United States tennis champion, Nancy Chafee, he vowed to his baseball buddies that he would beat his famous wife at tennis.

Well, Mr. and Mrs. Kiner started to play, and after being married six months, Ralph never lost a set at tennis by a score worse than 6-2. After one year of marriage, he never lost a set to his wife by a score worse than 6-4. After a year and one-half of marriage, his wife beat him by a score of no worse than 7-5.

Then it finally happened. There came a day when Ralph Kiner beat his famous wife at tennis, winning no less than two straight sets.

Happily, he informed his baseball buddies of the great tennis feat he had accomplished. However, when pressed for full details of his tennis victory over his wife, he reluctantly and somewhat embarrassedly confessed:

"Well, fellers, you see, she had a bad day when I licked her. She's only eight months pregnant."

☆ ☆ ☆

On May 2, 1954, Hall-of-Famer Stan Musial had the most awesome batting day ever achieved by a major-league player. In a doubleheader against the New York Giants, he walloped five home runs. It was the most ever hit by a big-league batter in a single day of major-league baseball.

When the happy Stan Musial returned to the clubhouse, following his fantastic hitting feat, to receive the acclaim that was due him, the first to greet him was his twelve-year-old son, with the comment: "Gee, Dad, that's some crummy pitching staff the Giants have to let you hit five homers."

☆ ☆ ☆

Long before quarterback Joe Namath became pro football's most glamorous hero by leading the 1968 New York Jets to a Super Bowl victory and the football championship of the world, he never sold himself short as a gridiron great.

One Saturday afternoon when he was the quarterback for the University of Alabama, in a game against Auburn, Joe handed off to one of his running backs. However, the runner was brought down so viciously on the play that when it ended, a couple of Alabama and Auburn players began throwing fists. A near-riot ensued.

As the brawl was squashed, one of the officials charged into the midst of the milling players in an attempt to fix the blame for that fight. Since he was new to the Southeastern Conference, he was not familiar with the names of the players.

He spotted quarterback Joe Namath, and he snapped at him: "Are you Wright?" Apparently, the official had confused him with his fighting teammate, Frank Wright.

Whereupon Joe Namath, a native of Beaver Falls, Pennsylvania, drew himself up to his full height of 6-feet-2 inches, and drawled in his best affected Southern accent: "Suh, a Namath is always right!"

The confused official was so awed by Joe Namath's haughty reply that he promptly ordered play to be resumed without penalizing anyone.

☆ ☆ ☆

Once during a tense, rough and brawling hockey game, courageous Camille Henry, one of the tiniest players in the National Hockey League, lost his temper and tangled with big tough defenseman Fernie Flaman, one of the most feared battling sluggers in the league. As they grappled, shoulder to shoulder, pint-sized Henry suddenly shouted a warning at his huge opponent who outweighed him by more than fifty pounds:

"Watch out, Fernie, or I'll bleed all over you!"

☆ ☆ ☆

Before Detroit's Denny McLain became the most famous pitcher of the major leagues by winning thirty-one games during the 1968 season, he spent some time in the minor leagues, learning his trade.

He tells a story about a team that used addition signs for its pitchers. The catcher would pump one finger, then pump one finger again, and then flash three fingers. The key to the signal for the pitcher was the first two pumps. The hurler on the mound had to add them together to get the right pitch called for. But on one particular day, the rookie pitcher on the mound kept crossing up the catcher. Finally, the disgusted backstop went out to the mound, and snarled at the pitcher: "What's the matter, dope, can't you add?"

"Sorry," answered the rookie pitcher. "But try me on history. I was very good at that in school."

☆ ☆ ☆

When the little-known rookie Hank Aaron came up for his first time at bat in a major-league game, the rival catcher said to him mockingly: "Hey, kid, you're holding your bat all wrong. You should hold it with the label up so you can read it."

"I didn't come up here to read," retorted young Aaron. Fifteen years later, during the 1968 season, he became the eighth player in major-league history to hit more than 500 home runs, and he was still holding his bat wrong and going strong.

☆ ☆ ☆

On a post-season tour in the sticks, a bunch of major-leaguers found themselves playing a small-town outfit on a field surrounded by corn that ran all around the outfield.

"They'll beat the pants off us," said one of the major-leaguers. "If the ball ever gets into that corn, we're sunk."

"No, you're not," answered one of the coaches, handing him a sack of baseballs. "Go out there and plant these along the edge of the outfield when nobody's looking."

Seven surprised local baserunners were thrown out that day from the outfield.

In his early years as the head football coach of Notre Dame, the immortal Knute Rockne swore like a trooper during practice sessions with his team, even in the presence of the priests who dared to come and watch the players. One of the regular attendants at practice was the gentle Father Hennessy who had great influence over Notre Dame athletics. However, coach Rockne's sulphurous cussing never turned a hair on the good Father's head.

One afternoon, Rockne let fly with a particularly salty stream of oaths.

All eyes turned to the imperturbable Father Hennessy standing on the sidelines. There was no doubt that he had heard every syllable. The food Father merely sighed, raised his eyes heavenward, and said, loud enough for the coach to hear: "Oh, Glory be to God! There goes Mr. Rockne saying his prayers again."

Some years ago, one of America's greatest distance runners was Gil Dodds, famed as the Flying Parson. He was an ordained minister. One afternoon, after winning a record-smashing mile race against a highly touted runner, the "Flying Parson" was buttonholed by an inquisitive reporter who pressed him for an inside story on his victory.

"The Lord ran with me today," explained Gill Dodds modestly. The reporter then turned to the beaten runner, and asked: "And what happened to you? How do you explain your defeat?"

"It's very simple," snapped the badly beaten runner in disgust. "I had to run alone."

They say that an apple a day keeps the doctor away, but the immortal Babe Ruth, greatest home-run hitter of all time, never believed it.

The "King of Swat" was king-size in everything he did, even when it came to eating. He had a gargantuan appetite which he couldn't control even during working hours. Once, just before the start of a game, Babe sneaked in a couple of sandwiches, ate a dozen hot dogs, gulped down ten bottles of soda pop, and then topped off that hurried snack with an apple. After only a few innings of play, he caved in with a stomach-ache that was heard around the baseball world. Headlines told an entire nation about Babe Ruth's bellyache.

When the very sick and unhappy Babe was carted off to a hospital, he moaned: "I knew I shouldn't have et that apple."

⭐ ⭐ ⭐

The former famous major-league umpire Red Jones recalls the time he and an umpire friend were invited to lead a community sing at a church social. The preacher asked the congregation to turn to page forty-two. The two umpires sounded the first note in their deep baritone voices, but suddenly, both shut their mouths, and no sound came forth. For when the two umpires scanned the pages, they noted the name of the hymn was "Open Thine Eyes."

☆  ☆  ☆

When Charlie Moran was a famous umpire in the major leagues, he also was a well-known breeder of hunting dogs. One afternoon he was umpiring at home plate in a game between the Chicago Cubs and the Cincinnati Reds, when second baseman Hughie Critz, a notoriously weak hitter, came to bat for his first time. He promptly brought up the subject of hunting dogs.

"Got any good ones for sale?" he asked umpire Moran.

"Sure do! I've got a good one for one hundred and fifty dollars," replied the ump, as he called the first pitch a ball.

"That's a lot of money," protested batter Critz.

"Not for the best hound dog you can buy," snapped umpire Moran as he called the second pitch a ball.

"That dog fast?" asked the batter.

"He'll run right past any rabbit," replied the ump, as he called the third pitch a ball.

"Can he retrieve?" asked Hughie Critz.

"Through brimstone and high water," replied the ump.

"I'll buy him!" said the batter.

"Ball four!" snapped umpire Charlie Moran, waving Hughie Critz to first on a walk.

That was too much for the famous Gabby Hartnett, catching for the Cubs. He turned and roared angrily at the startled ump:

"Moran, this is neither the time nor place to peddle your lousy hound dogs! And next time, don't you sell any of your hound dogs to a lousy .200 hitter!"

☆  ☆  ☆

Unquestionably, the most traveled player in big-league history was the one-time colorful Louis "Bobo" Newsom, who in nineteen seasons pitched for fifteen teams in both major leagues. Nevertheless, he won more than two hundred games, and he was a World Series hero, too. He was also celebrated as a merry clown who was quick with an amusing answer in defense of his faults and vices.

That wandering character had a weakness for the horses. A baseball day rarely passed when Bobo failed to place a bet on a horse race. Eventually, the famous iron-fisted Czar of Baseball, the late Judge Kenesaw Mountain Landis, who abhorred gambling in any form, heard about Bobo's vice, and he promptly called him up on the carpet for a judicial accounting.

"Look here, Newsom," snapped the stern Baseball Commissioner, "a ballplayer who bets on race horses can't keep his mind on the game! Suppose you're pitching in a tight ballgame and have to go to bat in the eighth inning when you've got a big bet going on a horse. What will you be thinking of then, baseball or your bet?"

Pitcher Bobo Newsom looked the tough Judge squarely in the eye, and squashed him with a direct and honest reply:

"Mr. Commissioner, you don't have to worry about that. If it's a tight ballgame in the eighth, it's a sure bet Ol' Bobo won't be in there batting!"

☆ ☆ ☆

Once there was a ballplayer who made a triple play, but the record books have neglected to list the glory of that moment. It was the most amusing triple play ever made.

It happened years ago when Larry McLean was a famous major-league catcher. In those days, Larry McLean was also a fast-stepping playboy. One afternoon, he showed up for a game, looking quite woozy and ragged, after a big night of merrymaking. It developed into a close game, and after a few innings of crouching behind the plate, under the hot sun, poor Larry McLean was in a daze, playing purely by instinct. Came a late inning, and the shaky and woozy Larry McLean let a pitch dribble out of his mitt. Hastily throwing off his mask, he pounced on the ball, and whirled just in time to see an enemy runner trying to come home from third. Larry McLean dashed for the plate to cut off the runner, and he arrived at home plate at the same time the umpire did, as did his pitcher who had raced in from the mound to cover the unprotected home plate. Seeing everything in a haze, catcher Larry McLean saw three men closing in on home plate, so without stopping to choose, the big catcher, with the ball gripped in his big fist, tagged the runner, the umpire, and his own pitcher.

"I don't know who the runner is," he shouted, "but I made a triple play, and one of you guys is out!"

☆ ☆ ☆

One of the most famous umpires in baseball history was the colorful Henry "Steamboat" Johnson. Tough and witty, he was never at a loss to know what to say or do in defense of his dignity and authority — except once. It happened when he was assigned to officiate in his first Ladies' Day game.

On that memorable day, when he arrived at the ballpark, he was amazed to find it packed to the rafters with a wild crowd of screeching females. When he swaggered out on the field to begin officiating behind home plate, he was startled by his reception. For almost all the women in the stands stood up in a body to jeer at him.

Amused by his hostile reception, Steamboat Johnson walked up close to the stands, boldly faced the hooting mob of shrieking females, silenced them with a courtly bow, then boomed at them in his most gentlemanly voice: "Why, girls! I don't think we've been properly introduced."

Whereupon a huge and husky woman leaned over the grandstand rail, and broke her parasol over the famous umpire's head, as she shrieked with delight: "Well, we have now, Mr. Johnson!"

Early in his fabulous career, the unforgettable Snapper Garrison, probably the greatest jockey of them all, who made a "Garrison Finish" part of the American language, was bitterly berated one day by the disappointed owner of a horse which had lost a race. The young and inexperienced jockey almost had piloted that broken-down nag to a surprising victory when that 50-to-1 shot had faltered.

"You had the race in your pocket," shrieked the irate horse owner. "Why didn't you keep on going instead of folding up in the homestretch?"

"What?" snapped the Snapper. "And leave my horse?"

A dash of diplomacy is what a good umpire needs. The famous Red Oromsby had it when he officiated in the major leagues.

One day, he was having an exceedingly rough time umpiring at home plate. The partisan hometown rooters were heckling him on almost every pitch. In that hostile mob, his severest critic was a screaming female sitting not far from home plate. Her raucous voice was louder than all others.

Finally there came a lull in the storm of abuse. But suddenly the loud-mouthed female screeched at the top of her powerful lungs: "Oromsby, you stupid blind bum! If you were my husband, I'd give you poison!"

The harassed umpire slowly turned towards the grandstand, doffed his cap to the offending lady, and roared: "Madam, if you were my wife, I'd be most happy to take it!"

One hot afternoon umpire Bill Klem was behind the plate in a tight game being played between the Brooklyn Dodgers and the Pittsburgh Pirates. The bases were loaded, when George Grantham of the Pirates was called out on strikes. Angrily, the player turned on Klem and roared: "Bill, you're blind. That ball was outside a mile."

Being in a good mood, the witty Bill Klem smilingly replied: "I'll leave it to the Dodger catcher to say what it was."

Whereupon the Dodger catcher, Johnny Gooch, stood up and sneeringly said to Bill Klem: "Alibi your own lousy decisions. I've got troubles of my own."

Bill Klem lost his good mood, turned on the catcher and bellowed: "Another word out of you, and out of the game you go."

"I hope I do," replied catcher Gooch. "I've been trying to tell that dumb manager of mine that I've got a sore foot, but he won't listen."

Bill Klem didn't kick Gooch out of the game.

☆ ☆ ☆

A rooster who was strutting his stuff in a chicken yard that backed up to a football stadium was nearly frightened to death one afternoon when a football bounded over the fence and landed at his feet. After a few moments, the puzzled rooster sidled over to the pigskin. He took a few pecks at it and backed away hurriedly. Then he strutted back, pecked at it again, and made a couple of passes with his wings. Then he glared at it until he felt firmly convinced that what he saw was not a figment of his imagination. Satisfied at last, he rushed over to the henhouse and stuck in his head.

"Come on out here, girls," he chirped, "and make it snappy!" The hens filed out meekly and formed a semicircle around the rooster. "All right, now," continued the rooster, "listen to me! I don't mean to make any of you feel bad. You've been doing pretty good work, considering, but take a look at that"—and he indicated the football—"and see for yourselves what they're turning out in some of the other yards around here!"

☆ ☆ ☆

When Billy Evans, who was later a highly paid and highly respected baseball executive with the Detroit Tigers, made his debut as an umpire in the major leagues, the umpire-baiting brigade took a violent dislike to him because of the very first decision he made. It happened in the opening game of a new baseball season. Billy Evans called a close one against the home team. Down from the stands came a shower of garbage, overripe fruit and bottles. Frightened, the inexperienced young umpire quickly ran to the safety of the nearest dugout. After a lull, Billy Evans cautiously poked his head out and asked his umpire-mate, John Sheridan:

"Hey, John, is it safe to come out now?"

Snickering at the young umpire's timidity, the hard-boiled veteran roared:

"Come on out, you young squirt! This is only April. Wait until August, when these bums get the range."

At that moment, a bottle whizzed close to Billy Evans' head. Quickly, he ducked back into the dugout, as he screamed in fright:

"Th' hell you say! They're in condition right now. Those bums are pitching strikes."

☆ ☆ ☆

A certain fight manager who was notorious for his crookedness and mistreatment of his fighters walked into a little cafeteria near Times Square right after one of his boys had taken a terrible beating in the ring from an opponent who was much too good for him. The little character began to shoot his mouth off about what a wonderful guy he was and how much he had collected for the contest that evening. Not once did he mention the boy who still lay battered and bleeding on a table in a Madison Square Garden dressing room. The counterman looked at the mug with a sour expression and asked him what he wanted.

"Gimme a hunk o' apple pie," said the leech. "An' cawfee." He paused, then plunged. "And an order o' cheese."

The counterman nodded. "How'll ya have the cheese," he asked gently, "on the pie or in a trap?"

☆ ☆ ☆

Red Barrett, talkative pitcher of the old Boston Braves, who won his share of games with a mystifying nothing-ball, was telling some of the boys in the dugout about a hard-luck experience of his while pitching in the International League. It seems that the redhead had been blanking the old Baltimore Orioles for eight innings and had reached the last of the ninth, still holding a slim lead of 1-0.

"Then you know what happens?" continued the disgusted Barrett. "I got them two out and the bases full and that durn shortstop of mine picks up an easy roller and heaves it clean out of the park. That's hard luck for you!"

"Yeah," sympathized a teammate who had been listening closely, "but can I ask you something, Red?"

"Sure," answered the aggrieved Barrett.

"How did the bases get loaded in the first place?"

☆ ☆ ☆

Shortly after Knute Rockne was killed in an airplane crash, the Notre Dame Alumni Association decided to hold an impressive memorial ceremony on the South Bend campus, in loving memory of the immortal football coach of the Fighting Irish. The alumni officers thought it would be fitting on that important occasion to have present the oldest living alumnus of Notre Dame. So, the files were checked and it was discovered that the oldest graduate of that famed Jesuit institution had been a German-born student named Newmark, class of 1878. Upon further research, the alumni officials learned that this Newmark, now past 80 years old, was living at a certain address in Los Angeles, California. An invitation was mailed to him requesting his honored presence on the campus of Notre Dame—for the Knute Rockne ceremony. He responded with a brief letter. It read:

"I am unable to accept the invitation, for we old gaffers are forbidden to travel long distances. I must obey the rules if I am to remain living happily here—at the Jewish Home for the Aged."

☆ ☆ ☆

Not all rookies are naive and dumb. Some of them are fast on the draw with brain and tongue.

When Frankie Frisch was manager of the St. Louis Cardinals, he came into possession of a rookie infielder named Sam Narron. One morning in spring training camp, the playing manager of the Cards was on the sidelines, lazily leaning on a bat and watching his players going through their practice paces. Suddenly, his eagle eye spied rookie Sam Narron in a corner of the field, lazily leaning on a bat — loafing.

The fiery-tempered manager stopped all play, and with a sharp tongue berated the young rookie in the presence of all the players.

"What d'ya mean by loafing in the field?" roared Frisch. "Are you too stupid to understand my orders? Only this morning we had a clubhouse meeting and do you remember I told all young players that I wanted each one of them to pick out a star on the team and imitate him at all times? Well, you lazy bum, did you?"

"Of course, sir," the rookie replied politely. "I picked you!"

☆ ☆ ☆

While Larry Gilbert, popular manager of the old Nashville club, was noted for the consideration he showed his players, he found that it didn't always pay off to be nice to them. There was a pinch-hitter on his club who was cordially disliked by the fans. Gilbert found it necessary to use him once, and wishing to keep the fans off the poor guy, the manager left the dugout with him and accompanied him on the walk toward the batter's box. As soon as the two men stuck their heads out on the field, the hooting and yelling began, and the noise from the stands got louder and louder as they neared the plate.

"Don't mind 'em," said Gilbert soothingly to the hitter. "You know how fans are. You just smack one on the nose and you'll hear those howls change to cheers right away."

"You got it all wrong, boss," answered the pinch-hitter. "They ain't on me at all. They're giving you the bird for having the nerve to use me!"

☆ ☆ ☆

One spring when the Chicago White Sox were in training camp, the team acquired an eccentric left-handed pitcher from Texas named Pat Caraway. They brought him North, and one cold and blustery afternoon the Sox were playing an early-season game in the Windy City. Late in the game, the shivering rookie approached the manager.

"Kin Ah go home, boss?" he asked through chattering teeth.

"What for?" demanded the astonished manager.

"Ah'm cold, an' Ah forgot mah overcoat," replied the southpaw.

Since the game was nearly over, the manager saw no harm in humoring the eccentric youngster. Slapping him on the back, he said, "Sure, kid. Go ahead."

So the screwball pitcher scurried from the Chicago ball park and went all the way back home to Texas to get his overcoat.

☆ ☆ ☆

One spring training day in Florida the Giants were playing a tight and exciting exhibition game against a rival major-league team. Manager Bill Terry was howling for a victory. The players to a man were driving hard to satisfy their boss. In a late inning, the Giants started a rally. Manager Bill Terry pointed dramatically at Fresco Thompson who was sitting on the Giant bench.

"Go in there, Thompson, and run for that guy on second!" he yelled.

"Gee, boss, I can't," protested Thompson, "I just had my shoes shined."

☆ ☆ ☆

Boys will come to blows and so will ballplayers, which is no secret to any newspaperman who follows a baseball club. One of the best brawls that ever took place on a ball club was one that occurred many years ago on a railroad car when a National League team was on its way to New York to play an important series that would mean a great deal in the standings. For some reason or other, the tough manager of the team and his scrappy star pitcher tangled in the aisle of the car and the battle raged up and down between the seats for nearly half an hour. When it ended, the car was almost a wreck, and the two men were bruised, battered and bleeding. Exhausted with their efforts and nearly stripped to the waist, they sank into opposite seats and glared at each other. Suddenly the manager grinned through cracked lips.

"That reminds me," he said painfully, "I meant to tell you earlier that you're pitching the first game tomorrow."

☆ ☆ ☆

The great writer, Mark Twain, although no Willie Hoppe at billiards, nevertheless was one of the best amateur players of his time. He loved the game so much that he delighted in telling stories about his own prowess with the cue, even if the chuckle was on him.

"I was travelling in Nevada," tells the author of *Huckleberry Finn*, "and I dropped into a billiard parlor one day to pass a little time. Now,

I kind of fancied my skill with the cue in those days, and when a stranger came up to me offering to play me a game for a modest side bet, I figured I could take him on. I was choosing myself a nicely balanced stick when the stranger turned to me and said, with a trace of pity in his voice that I did not like, 'Pardner, I'll tell you what I'll do for you. I'm afraid your skill may not match mine, so I'll just play you left-handed.'

"That made me mad," continued Twain, "and I thought I had better give the churl a lesson. To begin with, we increased the bet to make it more interesting. Then we banked for first shot, this fellow shooting left-handed, as he promised, and he won. He started playing, still left-handed, of course, and I stood alongside the table chalking my cue and waiting for him to miss so I could take over and show him where he got off.

"Well, he played on and on and I just chalked and chalked. As a matter of fact, he ran out the game without even the hint of a miss. I paid the fellow, but I couldn't help being somewhat astonished. 'Gracious!' I exclaimed. 'If you're that good with your left hand, how well would you do shooting right-handed?'

" 'Wa-al,' replied the stranger to me as he tucked away his ill-gotten gains, 'mebbe not so good. After all, I *am* left-handed.' "

☆ ☆ ☆

☆ ☆ ☆

While Jake Ruppert owned the New York Yankees, one of his best scouts, Paul Krichell, discovered what he thought was a fine young prospect who also happened to be a preacher. He signed the boy to a contract, paid him $1000 on the spot, and then told him to report to one of the Yankee farm clubs.

Time passed and the promising rookie didn't show up. Inquiries failed to locate him anyplace. Colonel Ruppert sent for the scout and demanded an explanation. None was forthcoming.

"Look what you've done," mourned Ruppert. "You spent $1000 of my hard-earned money and what do I get for it? Eh, tell me!"

"Well, Colonel," answered the scout carefully, "there's always good will, you know. After all, the kid who's got your thousand bucks will sure be praying for you!"

☆ ☆ ☆

A jealous wife rummaged through her husband's pants pockets early one morning while he was still asleep and found a little black book in which was written the single entry, "Laura Kane, Central 721." She woke the guy up and stuck the little book under his nose.

"What does this mean?" she demanded.

"Laura Kane?" mumbled the sleepy spouse. "Oh, that's just the name of a horse I played yesterday."

"And what does Central stand for?"

"That's Central Avenue, honey, the street my bookie lives on."

"Uh, huh. And 721?"

"Why, sweetheart, that's just the odds on the horse. You know, seven to one."

While his wife was still wondering, the husband went back to sleep. An hour or so later she shook him vigorously by the shoulder.

"What's the matter now?" he demanded.

"Get up, you bum!" she snapped. "Your horse is on the phone!"

☆ ☆ ☆

A female golfer was having a bad time on the golf course. After flubbing an easy shot, she turned angrily on her snickering caddy. "If you don't stop that," she screeched, "you'll drive me out of my mind!"

"That wouldn't be no drive," answered the boy, "only a putt."

☆ ☆ ☆

During World War II a sports writer on one of our better journals grabbed an offer from his paper to turn foreign correspondent for the duration. He was assigned to the North African theatre. Being a bold and intrepid character, he decided to do a little snooping in the desert. The only transportation he could find was a moth-eaten and high-smelling camel.

At the end of the month, the sportswriter turned foreign correspondent sat down to make out his swindle sheet—expense account, that is— and having had many a row with the business office in former years, added as a joke the following item:

Purchased one racing camel for desert trip—$900.

When the expense account reached the auditor of the paper, that tough and hard-boiled crab merely ran a black line through the item and returned it unpaid. Undeterred, the foreign correspondent made out a new accounting for the business office. In this he entered the following item:

Sold, one camel—$915.

A couple of weeks later, the ex-sportswriter who had built up something of a reputation as a fancy juggler of the swindle sheet, received his regular paycheck. With it was a note of explanation from the auditor:

"We are deducting fifteen dollars from your pay check," it read. "As you are there in the employ of this newspaper, the profit you made from the sale of the camel belongs to us."

☆ ☆ ☆

George Earnshaw, a well-known Philadelphia right-hander of yesteryear, was pitching for Connie Mack's Athletics against the New York Yankees on a day when the famed Bronx Bombers of old were in a deadly slugging mood. Before a couple of innings had been played, Big George Earnshaw had more than his share of trouble for one baseball day.

Among his chief tormentors was the late Lou Gehrig, who in his first two times at bat had socked two home runs into the right-field stands.

After the second homer, manager Connie Mack lost his patience and faith and yanked the faltering pitcher out of the game. Disgusted with himself, Earnshaw started for the clubhouse but Connie Mack sharply called him back to the dugout and ordered him to sit down.

"You sit right here next to me for the rest of this game. I want you to watch how Mahaffey is going to pitch to that Gehrig fellow."

Earnshaw plunked down on the bench, resigned to watch his successor hurl against the rampaging Yankees. Presently, up to bat again came Lou Gehrig, and this time he pickled the first pitch into the left-field stands for another home run. There was a long and awkward silence finally broken by Earnshaw who turned to his manager and said:

"I see perfectly what you mean, Mr. Mack. He sure made Gehrig change the direction."

☆ ☆ ☆

A couple of sharp characters named Harry and Chick arrived at the racetrack loaded down with the usual paraphernalia of horseplayers, plus instruments to calculate wind drift and moisture in the air, a slide rule, six assorted scratch sheets, columns of figures, pads, pencils, and stop watches. They went right to work figuring the possibilities of the first race. After taking everything into account, including the age, weight, color and family connections of the stable grooms, they settled on the probable winner.

"I make it number seven," said Chick.

"Seven it is," answered Harry, and went off to make a sizable bet on their choice.

The race was run and number seven came in a flying eighth in an eight-horse field. In front of the two figure-filberts a little guy was jumping up and down like a monkey on a stick. As the red board flashed on, he turned to the two calculating demons and with a shining face said, "I had the winner, number nine. And look at the price, 12 to 1!"

As the little guy dashed off to the windows to collect his winnings, Harry looked at Chick. "Luck," he said with distaste, "just plain bone-head luck."

The two pals went back to work on the second race. Harry got out his pocket adding machine. After dividing the weight on the horses by the sizes of the jockeys' caps, they again agreed on the probable winner.

"Number four," said Harry.

"Check!" said Chick. And off he went to make an even bigger bet this time.

Number four trailed the field. The view of the race was ruined for the two buddies by the same little character in front of them who kept bobbing up and down and screaming all the while.

"I did it again!" screamed the little guy. "Another winner and a $19.70 mutuel!"

Harry leaned forward and tapped the little guy on the shoulder. "I don't get it," he said. "We figure and figure and figure and we can't find a winner. All you got is a program in your hand and you don't even bother to look at it to pick your horses. How do you do it?"

The little guy smiled. "I got me a system," he said. "Easy as pie.

All I do is pick the two best-looking horses in the parade before the race, add the numbers together, and play the total. Like in the last race, I see number three and number seven are the best-looking, so I go and play number nine. And number nine wins. See?"

Chick and Harry exchanged glances. "Look," said Chick gently to the excited little character, "three and seven add up to ten. You should have played ten, according to your figures."

"Figures, figures!" exploded the little guy in disgust. "You and your lousy figures!"

☆ ☆ ☆

The American Indian has been well represented in the field of sports in the United States. The Carlisle School, now only a memory, turned out famous athletes in track, baseball and football by the score. The Carlisle Indian football team left not only an indelible impression in the minds of all sports fans, but also a flock of stories that will never be forgotten.

When Glen "Pop" Warner was coach of the Carlisle Indians, he had an assistant by the name of Bunny Larkin, one-time college star. It was Larkin's job to explain the principles of football to the new candidates for the eleven. When the boys turned out for their first day of practice, Larkin lined them up before him. His explanation was brief and to the point.

"Boys," he said, "football is like this: When white man has ball, *knock down white man.* When Indian has ball, *knock down white man.*"

One year, the Carlisle Indians fielded a football team whose only fault was over-confidence and just a touch of laziness. The worst of these offenders was the big powerful guard, Black Bear. When aroused, Black Bear was the most devastating lineman ever seen on the gridiron. When let alone, he was the most good-natured, easygoing of men.

Carlisle's quarterback was Gus Welch, in the minds of many old-timers the greatest of them all. And Black Bear was his problem. Carlisle took the field against a strong fast Pennsylvania eleven. In no time at all, Welch was beside himself with rage as the big Penn backs began to tear great holes in the Carlisle line. Welch diagnosed the situation quickly. Black Bear was only going through the motions of playing football. After each big gain through him, Black Bear rose from the turf with a grin on his face as though nothing had happened.

It was more than Gus Welch could stand. On the next scrimmage, Black Bear was, as usual, at the bottom of a heap of players. Welch crept up behind the unsuspecting Black Bear and smashed him right on the ear.

Black Bear came to his feet with a roar. "Who hit me? Who hit me?"

he yelled. Welch pointed silently at the Penn players and walked away.

For the rest of the afternoon, the aroused Black Bear played like a demon possessed. He ripped the Penn line to shreds. Carlisle went on to victory.

Having learned how to get the best out of Black Bear, Welch never let up. In the next game—against Harvard—Gus managed to sink his teeth deep into the big guard's leg. That was the end of Harvard. Next time it was a well-placed kick. Then a punch. Then another punch. And so it went, right through the season.

Welch and Black Bear graduated from the Carlisle School together. On the last day there, the two teammates fell to talking about their experiences. Finally, Gus Welch asked, "Well, Black Bear, did you enjoy playing football?"

"Oh, sure," replied Black Bear, but then his face clouded. "But you know, Gus, I never once played in a game that some white man didn't play me dirty by sneaking in a punch or a bite in scrimmage!"

☆  ☆  ☆

Among the reporters waiting to greet the New York Yankees as they arrived at Grand Central sporting a 17-game winning streak some years ago, was a young cub who sought out and grabbed manager Joe McCarthy as he stepped off the train. "How do you do, Mr. McCarthy," said the youngster politely. "How are the Yankees going?"

Marse Joe tipped back his hat and looked down at the brash young man. "Well," he answered at last, "I guess you could quote me as saying that they're doing fairly well but there's room for improvement. You see, we're only licking one team at a time right now."

☆  ☆  ☆

A sports announcer broadcasting a baseball game in Brooklyn told his audience the news that Babe Herman had popped a fly to Don Hurst, thus:

"Hoiman hersted to Hoist."

☆  ☆  ☆

Sam Taub, well-known fight announcer during the broadcast of the Tony Zale-Rocky Graziano title battle, informed his audience thus:

"Zale has him in a neutral corner where it doesn't hurt."

☆  ☆  ☆

The crowd at Churchill Downs for the Kentucky Derby is one of the biggest ever assembled in the world of sports. It was so last May, and the May before, and as far back as anyone can remember. It was just as big in '38, when a fellow who had been too busy drinking mint juleps finally fought his way to the betting window with his two-dollar bill just as the wicket slammed down in his face.

"Hey, what's the idea?" growled the guy. "I wanna two-buck ticket on Fighting Fox."

"Too late, bud," said the clerk. "The race has started."

"Nuts to you," chirped the drunk. "This two-spot is as good as one of your old tickets, anyway." And, waving the two-dollar bill in his fist, he staggered back to the grandstand just as the horses came thundering past the finish line.

"Who won?" he asked a neighbor.

"Lawrin," was the answer.

"What about Fighting Fox?" asked the lush.

"He wasn't any place," answered the other.

"Oh, damn!" moaned the drunk. And he tore the two-dollar bill into little pieces.

☆ ☆ ☆

A handful of disgruntled fans sat in the stands to welcome home a ragged and worn-out band of major-league ballplayers who had just finished spring training without a single victory, not even over their lowliest farm clubs. As the players lined up at home plate for the traditional march to the flagpole for the raising of Old Glory, the muttering in the stands grew louder and louder. As they approached the closed double-doored exit gate near which rose the flagpole, one fan could stand the pain of it all no longer. He leaped to his feet and, in a voice of anguish, cried, "Open the gate, somebody! Open the gate and let the poor slobs keep marching!"

☆ ☆ ☆

It was May 30th, a hot sunny day. The great stadium was jammed to the distant fences with shirt-sleeved fans who waited patiently for the big fight to begin. In the center of the ring stood the immaculately-garbed announcer, his gleaming white jacket setting off his neatly pressed dark trousers and his sleek well-groomed hair. Suddenly an invisible band swung into the stirring strains of the national anthem. The crowd rose solemnly and listened to the song that means so much on this day of sad remembrance of our war dead. Then, in dead silence, they sat down. The announcer in the ring reached for his microphone. "Ladies and gentlemen!" he cried, and his melodious voice carried to the farthest reaches of the great arena. "Before we commence the business of the afternoon, let me wish you all a happy Memorial Day!"

That was Harry Balogh, announcer extraordinary, the man with more words than the dictionary because he made up a lot of them himself. Who had ever heard Harry Balogh's last words to a pair of fighters in the ring and not been touched to the very core of his being by them? They will ring forever from the rafters of Madison Square Garden, no matter where Harry Balogh goes. "And may the better adversary emerge triumphant from this combat!" Stirring words! Or, "May the arm of the better participant be elevated in token of victory!"

A fighter who had earned Harry's admiration because he had always met all challengers was likely to be introduced by him as follows: "Introducing a man who bars, and never has barred, anyone regardless of

99

race, creed or color." Or if it happened to be a fighter worthy of the highest praise, Harry may have presented him as he once did Gus Lesnevich: "Introducing Les Gusnevich who, like good wine, goes on forever!"

Once he introduced that great favorite of fight fans, Barney Ross, as a "former" native of New York. It is to be doubted that Barney, who had been born in New York, had moved his birthplace elsewhere.

On the night of a certain important fight, an emergency telephone call to the arena was relayed immediately to Harry Balogh in the ring. Harry raised his arm for silence. The crowd, though impatient for the big fight to begin, became still. Harry waited and the suspense became unbearable. At last he deigned to speak.

"Is Joe Smith of New Rochelle in the crowd? Joe, I regret that I am obliged to inform you that we have just received word that your dear mother suffered a serious stroke within the past hour. Our deepest sympathy goes out to you, Joe. Be a good boy, a fine son, and a real sport. Go out and call her right up. Then come back and enjoy the fight!"

A reporter, deeply affected by one of Harry's most stirring elocutionary exhortations, made by the announcer on the spur of the moment, leaned forward into the ring and addressed the wordy windbag. "Harry," he asked, "did you really extemporize that speech?"

"Hell, no," answered Balogh, "I made it up as I went along."

Early in his career, Harry was announcing in a small club. In the far distant fifty-cent seats a pesky fan kept howling all evening, "I want blood! Give me blood!" At last, Harry stepped out and raised his hand. "Quiet, please!" he shouted. "There will be no transfusions given for fifty cents!"

Harry often functioned in his wonted capacity at charity affairs for which he refused to accept a cent of payment. It was on one such occasion that he made his most priceless contribution to the art of garbled speech. The affair was being run for a very worthy charity but, oddly enough, the fight had attracted a most plebeian crowd of roughnecks. Harry spieled the mob for twenty eloquence-drenched minutes with the most soul-lifting appeal for contributions ever heard anywhere. At its close, he waved his arm to indicate the group of pretty young debutantes who stood waiting for his signal to go out and collect the offerings from the crowd.

"There they are!" shouted Harry in his most persuasive tones. "Get yourselves ready, gentlemen! These lovely young society maidens with their little 'cans' are about to pass among you. Please—please take good care of them!"

☆ ☆ ☆

Don't know why, but most fisherman are fantastic liars.

Two fishermen were spinning tales of their recent catches. Said one: "Last week I caught a three-hundred-pound salmon." To which the second fisherman replied:

"Bah, that's impossible! Salmon never weigh three hundred pounds."

"Mine did!" roared the first fisherman stubbornly.

"Well," drawled the second fisherman, "I wasn't going to tell you this, but last week I was fishing and I pulled up an old lantern. There was a tag on it, too, and it said that the lantern had been dropped into the water back in 1910, but even stranger than that, believe it or not, the light inside the lantern was still lit."

Whereupon the first fisherman sighed wearily and said:

"My friend, let's get together on these stories. I'll take a hundred pounds off my fish if you'll put the light out in that lantern."

The famous Tommy Hitchcock, America's greatest polo player, shortly before he was killed in World War II, while he was stationed in England, engaged in a polite argument with a famous British sportsman about the snobbishness and democracy as practiced by the athletes from both countries.

"We're far more democratic in American sports than you Englishmen are over here," stoutly insisted Tommy Hitchcock. "I maintain that all you English sportsmen are much too reserved."

101

"Sheer nonsense!" retorted the Britisher indignantly, "Why, take me for an example. I'm the son of a duke, yet when I was in Oxford and rowing on my college eight, I knew all the other chaps on the crew quite well except one—but he was way up in the bow."

Dink Templeton, famous track coach, was watching a college meet on the West Coast one day when an eager-eyed young man in track clothes edged over to him timidly.

"Mr. Templeton," said the youngster, "I run the hundred but I'm not satisfied with the time I make. How can I improve it?"

"That's easy," grunted Templeton, "just run faster."

☆ ☆ ☆

The excited Washington coach watched an Oregon back intercept a pass and start down the near sideline towards the Washington goal. "No! No!" he screamed in anguish. "Don't let him get away! Somebody stop him! Stop him! Oh, isn't there anybody who'll stop him?"

"There sure is, coach!" shouted one of the Washington substitutes from his place near the frantic coach. "I will!" And with that, the splinter-ridden youth leaped from his seat and tackled the enemy runner as he sped past.

A certain riot was narrowly averted when Washington hastily conceded the touchdown to the thwarted Oregonians.

☆ ☆ ☆

The legend that lies behind Joe Jackson's nickname of "Shoeless" is as amusing as it is probably untrue. It is a fact that Joe went barefoot most of his youth as most poor boys in the South did. But he is reputed to have played baseball barefoot, too. When Joe started out in baseball before coming up to the big time, he found himself playing one afternoon on a field that was littered with garbage like a city dump. He had to climb over heaps of trash and debris to reach his position and then plow through the junk to cover his position.

After several innings had been played, Joe came in from the outfield quite perturbed. Spotting the owner of the local club, Joe buttonholed him. "Say, Mister," complained Joe, "you ought to clean up them broken bottles in the outfield."

The owner looked down at Joe's bare feet in amazement. "You crazy hillbilly," he exclaimed, "why don't you wear shoes to protect your feet?"

"Oh, I ain't worryin' about my feet," declared Joe earnestly. "That broken glass is ruinin' the covers of the baseballs!"

☆ ☆ ☆

The fact that Shoeless Joe was illiterate became known to the fans right away. One fat, red-faced character began to heckle Joe about it when the White Sox came to Cleveland for a series. Every time Joe came to bat, this fat fellow cupped his hands to his mouth and yelled, "Hey, Joe, how do you spell ignoramus?"

Jackson came up for the last time with a man on first and the score tied. Again the rude character in the stands shouted at him, "Hey, Joe, how do you spell ignoramus?"

Joe ignored him, or seemed to ignore him. He lined the first pitch to the deepest right-center for a triple, sending home the tie-breaking run. Standing on third base, Joe turned toward the stands. "Hey, Fatso!" he shouted. "How do you spell triple?"

☆ ☆ ☆

Long before Jackson became entangled in the Black Sox scandal that gave birth to the classic remark, "Say it ain't so, Joe," he was just a simple nobody in a little South Carolina backwoods community. One morning, a Sunday it was, the minister of the local church saw Joe walking along the road in a ragged baseball uniform. The minister, disapproval in every line of his face, stopped the young man.

"Look here, my boy," he boomed, "don't you know it's a sin to work on the Lord's day?"

"Shucks, Rev'rend," replied the unabashed Joe Jackson, "you don't mind workin' on Sunday, do you?"

"Of course I don't!" retorted the minister. "But remember, my son, when I work on Sunday, I am in the right field."

"Well, I'll be doggoned!" exclaimed the surprised youngster. "That's jes' whar they put me—in right field! Rev'rend, I'd sure be obliged if you'd give me a few pointers on playin' out thar!"

☆ ☆ ☆

When Joe came up to the majors, he could not make head or tail of a box score. However, he finally and with great difficulty learned how to read them, and kept track of his hitting and fielding as well as anybody.

One year, Jackson was in a hot race with the redoubtable Ty Cobb for the batting championship of the American League. After a game one evening, Joe bought a paper to examine the box score. He let out a roar of outrage.

"Looka here," he shouted. "They only give me one hit. I know I had a double and a single!"

The newsstand clerk looked at the box score over Joe's shoulder. "It's all right, Joe," he said. "That's probably only a typographical error."

"Typographical error, nothin'," growled Shoeless Joe. "It was as clean a hit as you ever want to see. Why, not a fielder came close to touchin' that ball!"

☆ ☆ ☆

It was a great day for the Irish, that day when the one and only John L. Sullivan graciously agreed to attend the annual picnic of the Ancient Order of Hibernians in the now busy city of North Adams, Mass. No man stood higher in the esteem of his fellow man than the Boston Strong Boy, and by the hundreds they pressed forward to shake the hand of the world's heavyweight champion. For it was the boast those days to top all boasts if one could say, "Here, friend, shake the hand that shook the hand of John L. Sullivan."

Beer flowed like—well, beer, and the spirits of the gathered Hibernians soared to the very sky as John L. entered the ring that had been set up on the side of a hill. Then it was that a flash of inspiration struck full upon the brow of a little man who hovered at ringside and worshipfully ogled his hero above him. What now, thought this little man. Shall I shake his hand and be like all the others? No, no. If I could but smite the champion—ah, then would I be indeed someone!

Suiting the action to the word, the little man sprang into the ring and swung mightily from his heels. The great John L. took the puny blow on his ribs and brushed the little man aside as though he were a mosquito.

Word of the little man's feat soon spread through the assemblage. In a trice the ring was full of Hibernians laying on with a will. John L. Sullivan retreated a step or two, then began to defend himself against the onslaught. Around him in piles lay such as were unfortunate enough to feel the ponderous weight of the great man's fists.

Then an odd thing happened. The hundred or so men in the ring began to fight each other. For, each man having struck his blow so that he could say, "Shake hands with the man who struck the mighty John L," there was now no need to attack him further. It was now important to keep others from attacking him, too.

104

So on and on went the melee until with a thunderous crash, the ring and its platform collapsed to the ground. But nothing stopped the ebb and flow of battle. When dark mercifully fell, John L. crawled out of the bloody hassle and quietly stole away, leaving behind him the crash and thud of continuing conflict.

Never again did the great John L. return to that enterprising city of North Adams. But he did not need to. The memory of his visit will be green till the world comes to an end.

☆　☆　☆

Most active of participants, Chet Miller drove his gasoline-buggy sixteen times in the famed annual Indianapolis Speedway classic before death caught up with him. He was killed trying to qualify on the eve of the 1953 race. Up to then, his escapes from destruction were little short of miraculous.

During the Indianapolis 500-mile race in 1934, Chet was winging along at 115 miles per hour when suddenly his car skidded on an oil patch, whirled into the air, and catapulted over the retaining wall as 100,000 spectators screamed with horror.

By some miracle, Miller's car landed squarely on its four wheels on the front lawn of a neat little stucco house outside the speedway. A white-haired lady who had been sitting on the porch rose to her feet and shook her tiny fist at the driver in the racing car.

"You get off my lawn!" she shrieked. "You careless drivers just plain make me sick. If you don't leave immediately, I'll have you arrested for reckless driving!"

"Sorry, ma'am," said Chet Miller meekly. And he backed off the lawn and drove his battered car around to the entrance to the Speedway.

☆ ☆ ☆

If you don't think there are any hazards to playing the game of baseball, think again after reading this story. The Philadelphia Athletics, in the good old days when Connie Mack really had a team of giants, were working their way east after spring training in California, and stopped in a small town in Colorado to play an exhibition game against the local club. The field on which the game was played consisted of a diamond set in the great open spaces. In the outfield, without a fence to back him up, was Eddie Collins. In the last inning, with the score tied, one of the local heroes got hold of a pitch and drove a high fly that soared a few feet over Eddie's head. The runner pattered around the bases as the ball sailed out into space, one eye cocked on Collins to see whether he was going to make the catch. Collins was a step short of making an easy catch when he suddenly stopped in mid-stride and backed away, and the ball landed in the sand and began to roll. Instead of trying to retrieve the ball, Collins walked gingerly towards the infield as the runner put on an extra burst of speed and slammed over the plate with the winning run.

Connie Mack stopped Collins as he came into the dugout. "What happened?" he asked gently. "Lose it in the sun?"

"No," answered Collins.

"Mebbe you lost your footing in that awful sand?" asked the sympathetic Mack.

"Nope," replied Eddie.

"Misjudge the ball?" persisted Mack.

"No."

"Well," demanded the by-now exasperated manager, "why didn't you at least try to pick it up?"

"Would you," asked Collins scornfully, "if there was a great big rattlesnake between you and the ball?"

☆ ☆ ☆

At Ebbets Field, where everything used to happen, the public address announcer to a hushed audience: "A small boy has been found lost."

☆ ☆ ☆

Another baseball broadcaster on the subject of weather: "Folks, the temperature is 42 and there's a drizzle falling. Here comes the umpire. He's dusting off the plate."

☆ ☆ ☆

Another sports announcer describing a play: "And there's a well-smacked ball going out into center field! And — it's curving foul!"

In his last year in baseball, Babe Herman spits on his hands as he comes to bat. An ever-faithful fan, loyal to the last: "Nice spit, Babe!"

A headline about an inimitable character after he was struck by a pitched ball:

DIZZY DEAN'S HEAD X-RAYED;
REVEALS NOTHING.

George Washington, the first President of the United States, was fond of horses. He raised them, bred them, and raced them. He also lost with them—and a lot of money went with them.

One day, in his infinite wisdom, George Washington decided he had enough. He sold his horses and vowed that he would never make another bet on a race.

You may be sure that George Washington kept his word and never again bet on a horse race. In fact, he reformed himself to the point where he not only stopped raising thoroughbred horses, but turned his attention to a different field of breeding altogether—he started raising MULES!

☆   ☆   ☆

A racetrack tout, down on his luck and without a thin dime to his name, was standing outside the gate to Belmont Park, and wondering how in the world he was going to manage to get in to conduct his nefarious business. He had been having a miserable run of luck and he was beginning to contemplate the relative pleasures of suicide when a well-dressed stranger suddenly tapped him on the shoulder.

"I have an extra clubhouse ticket," said the stranger. "Would you care to be my guest?"

After making sure that the stranger was flesh and blood and not an angel in disguise, the tout readily accepted. When they were comfortably seated, the tout addressed his host cautiously. "You like to bet, sir?" he asked.

"When I have a decent tip," replied the well-dressed gentleman.

The tout pulled himself together and went to work. "I'll tell you," he whispered, "it's only because you've been so kind that I can pass this along. I have a very strong line into one of the stables starting a horse in the first race, and I have been assured that it can't miss. Now, if you will bet a few bucks for me when you bet for yourself, I'll be glad to give you this sure thing."

The stranger agreed with enthusiasm. He bet a thousand dollars for himself and a hundred for the tout.

Unfortunately, the tout's luck was still bad, and the horse ran out of the money.

"Sorry," said the tout, "but did you see how that dog crossed over on our horse just when he was ready to make his move? I got a much better tip on the next race if you're still willing to bet."

Again the well-heeled stranger agreed, to the shocked surprise of the tout. Again he wagered a thousand dollars for himself and a hundred for the tout.

But again, the beast ran far out of the money. Strangely enough, the soft touch had no complaint to make and the tout kept after him on the same basis through the rest of the card. Eight races were played and on each race one hundred dollars ran for the tout. To the tipster's amazement, never a squawk came from his host, who had dropped eight thousand dollars.

After the last race the stranger invited the tout to dinner and a show. "You've had a bad day," he sympathized, "so please accept my hospitality this evening. And tomorrow we will come back to Belmont and try again."

The tout had a big time with his generous host and left him late in the evening after promising to meet him again the next afternoon. On his way home the tout ran into an old friend and confederate. To him he spilled the whole story. "Just think of it," he said in wonder, "the guy blows eight thousand clams for himself and eight hundred for me, and he still wants me to go back and try again tomorrow. What a lousy break! All that dough I got riding for me and I don't go to the windows once to collect."

"Brother," said the tout's colleague, "get rid of that no-good guy. He's hard luck."

☆ ☆ ☆

It was a fine spring morning, and Mrs. Blank surveyed the scene from her window with pleasure. Her glance fell to the street and she noticed a poorly-dressed man standing near the corner. Just then a man stopped and handed him a bill.

"I can do that, too," murmured Mrs. Blank to herself, "poor fellow might be starving."

She got an envelope, stuck a couple of dollars into it, and waved to the man. He came over to the window and she dropped the envelope into his hand. "Good luck!" she cried, and slammed the window shut.

The next day she was back at the window. There was the poorly dressed man again, walking up and down as though he were waiting for her. As soon as he caught sight of her, he beckoned to her to come down.

"Go ahead and help somebody," said Mrs. Blank to herself in vexation, "and see what you get for it." But then she thought better of it, and went downstairs to see what the fellow wanted. As she got to the street, the man thrust a well-filled envelope at her.

"Here's your $76," he said. "Good Luck paid 38 to 1. Who gave you that tip, anyhow?"

This was Bernie Bierman's classic jest in answer to the question so frequently thrown at him by marvelling football fans.

"How do I get such big men for my Minnesota teams?" began Bernie. "I'll tell you, my friend. I go driving out along a country road until I see a boy walking behind a plow. I stop and ask him the way to Minneapolis. If he leaves the plow and points the way for me with his finger, I thank him and drive on. But if he picks up the plow and uses it for a pointer, that's my man! I just load him in the car with me and bring him right to the registrar's office!"

☆ ☆ ☆

Jim Tatum, coach of the powerful University of Maryland football team, got a laugh from the fans when he publicly and in dead seriousness accused the very proper members of the Ivy League of recruiting— not big well-muscled footballers, but *honor* students!

The incident recalls a remark once made by the gloomy but capable Gilmour Dobie when he first came to coach football at Cornell in 1920. Dobie had been coaching at the University of Washington and at Annapolis where he had turned out a series of powerhouses that made phenomenal records.

Dobie stepped out of Lower Alumni Field for the first day of practice, and the Big Red candidates came pouring out of the locker rooms under Schoellkopf Field. The dour Scot took one look at the young hopefuls bearing down on him and let out a groan of despair.

"My gracious," he exclaimed. "I've got nothing but students!"

☆ ☆ ☆

It seems that a couple of neighboring towns had baseball teams which met every year. The rivalry was intense and a lot of money was bet on the outcome of the games. One year the teams were unusually well matched, and the contest came down to the home half of the ninth with the score knotted at 0-0. The first two batters went harmlessly out, but the next man really tucked into one and drove a screaming line drive towards deepest center field. Just as it was about to clear the fence to give the home team a hard-earned victory, the ball suddenly split in two. One-half kept going and disappeared over the fence. The other half hesitated in midair, then dropped into the eager and reaching hands of the visitors' center fielder.

As though at a signal, all eyes turned on the horrified umpire. That poor fellow, the only arbiter in the game, stood stockstill and as white as a sheet. The members of both teams converged on him. The fans began to spill over the rails of the stands by the hundreds. In a minute, the field was a mass of humanity, with the umpire swallowed up in the middle of it. Everybody was yelling at him to make a decision. What was it? A home run? The third out?

"I never seen such a thing," he finally said slowly. "I got to think this over."

"How much time do you need?" someone asked.

The umpire squeezed his eyes shut and tried to remember when his train was due to leave town. "Tell you what," he said, "come to my hotel round seven-thirty tonight and I'll have it all figured out for you."

The crowd dispersed and the umpire rushed back to his hotel, packed his bag, and made a bee-line for the station. The room clerk, however, was a home-town rooter, knew what had happened, and started telephoning. The crowd reached the station just in time to see the umpire jump on the train. As it began to move away, he waved to the howling mob from the back platform, his face wreathed in smiles. "I got it, folks," he shouted after them. "The home team wins, 1/2 to 0!"

☆ ☆ ☆

The late W. C. Fields, famous stage and movie comedian, took up the game of golf when he was at the height of his fame. Being an expert billiard player, he figured that golf would be a cinch. However, after a few months, the various intricacies of the game began to get under his skin.

One day, he was engaged in a match against another duffer. Fields was playing, if possible, a little worse than usual. As the score mounted, so did his temper. Finally he came to a water hole. Fields took dead aim at the elusive little pellet, swung with all his might, and poked it right into the drink.

Promptly he whirled on his opponent, ready to throw the blame on him for his bad luck. To the comedian's chagrin, he found that worthy gentleman standing quite motionless, with not even a smile on his face. Baffled for the moment, Fields decided to vent his wrath on his luckless caddy instead. He whirled on the boy who was innocently leaning against a golf bag behind the tee.

"Boy!" snapped Fields. "What's the idea of standing in back of me and getting me nervous? Move over there!" And he pointed to a spot some ten yards to the left. The caddy dutifully moved to the spot indicated. W. C. Fields addressed a fresh golf ball, swung, connected, and again watched the pill plop smack into the water. This time his rage blazed into angry fury as he spun on his heel and glared at his caddy. "Why are you standing over there?" screamed Fields. "You're in my line of vision, boy! Go stand over there!" And the comedian, surprisingly enough, indicated the identical spot on which the caddy had stood originally.

The caddy shook his head sadly and went back to his former position. But Fields was not through with him. "What are you mumbling, boy?" he barked.

"N-nothing," stammered the boy. "I was only standing where you told me to."

"Never mind what I told you!" roared W. C. Fields. "You do as I tell you!"

☆ ☆ ☆

Who will ever forget good old Uncle Wilbert Robinson and those daffy Dodgers he managed for eighteen hilarious years from 1914 to 1931? If you were a Brooklyn rooter and got sore over dropping a game that should have been won, did you have to drown your sorrows and keep your broken heart to yourself? No, all you had to do was reach for the phone and get good old Uncle Robbie into an argument on the other end. He would talk to you as long as you wanted to and try to make you see the error of your ideas. Anybody could talk to Robbie—cabdrivers, housewives, schoolboys—but nobody could talk him down or make him change his mind.

Nobody, that is, but Mrs. Robinson. She was the only person in the world Uncle Robbie feared or would listen to with respect. "Maw," as he called her, hadn't lived with the rotund little manager all those years without having learned a great deal about baseball. The worst part of his day when the Dodgers lost was when Uncle Robbie got home and the missus pinned his ears back for his faulty strategy. "You blew that one," Maw would say. "You should have done this, you should have done that."

Then, one day, Robbie surprised everybody by starting a green young rookie in the box in an important game against the Chicago Cubs. The poor kid took a fearsome shellacking, but Uncle Robbie just leaned back in the dugout having a fine old time for himself, his big middle shaking and his face beaming with undisguised pleasure. Finally the rookie was relieved and Robbie strolled over to Maw's box.

"There," he said, "I started the kid just like you wanted me to. Now I hope you're satisfied. Maybe you won't be so anxious to second-guess me again." Then, when Maw had nothing to say, he chuckled and came back to the bench. "Let that be a lesson to you, boys," he announced triumphantly. "The woman doesn't live who can tell a man how to play baseball!"

Show a manager a youngster who can pitch a winning game and he'll grin with pure happiness. Show him the pitcher who can shut out the opposition and he'll consider getting the guy a raise. But show him the fellow who can throw a no-hitter and—well, just look at what can really happen.

Some years ago, in a class D league, the home club sent a youngster named Cannonball Johnson to the mound. The kid was keyed up with excitement. His girl was in the stands rooting for him. A big-league scout was looking on. The kid was determined to make a big impression.

The umpire yelled "Play Ball!" Cannonball reared back and let fly with his fast one. There was a crack of the bat, and the ball sailed on a line far out to left field. The left fielder turned his back and began to run at top speed. Ball and fielder reached the fence at the same instant. There was a tremendous crash. The fielder crumpled on the grass, the ball still tight in his grip. They pried it loose, and carried the unconscious player from the field. A new man was sent in, and Cannonball sighed with relief. "That was a close one," he said to himself. "But it's the first out. The hardest one, they always say."

What followed would have been unbelievable to the onlookers if they hadn't been there to see it with their own eyes. Infielders tumbled and spilled all over the diamond to make miraculous stops and catches. Out-fielders scraped shins on concrete and elbows on iron rails to make breathtaking catches. One thrill topped another. It was fantastic.

But no one got on base against Cannonball Johnson. Out after out was registered on some of the most remarkable plays seen anywhere.

By the time eight innings had been played, another outfielder, the first baseman, and two catchers had been carried from the field, as well as three spectators who had almost been decapitated by line drives.

Now, in the ninth, Cannonball needed but three more outs. On the first pitch, the centerfielder slid ten feet on his stomach to catch a low line drive. After repair, he resumed play. The next pitch was hit back at the third baseman who was carried halfway out to left field by the impact. But he held on to the ball. Two out, and only one more man stood between the embattled Cannonball Johnson and immortality.

Cannonball wound up carefully. He threw with all his might. The ball sped to the plate waist high and right over the middle. The batter swung with a mighty cut. A streak of white flew from his bat. Cannonball saw a blur and instinctively turned his head away. The ball hit him glanc-ingly on the back of the skull and skidded off to the right. The first baseman flung up his arm to ward off the blow and the ball thudded into his glove. It was the third out. Cannonball Johnson had pitched a perfect no-hit, no-run game!

The next morning Cannonball appeared bright and early in his man-ager's office. "Well, boss," he shouted as he burst in, "did I impress the scout? Is he going to sign me to a major-league contract? Where do I report? When do I leave?"

"That scout wouldn't touch you with a ten-foot pole!" roared the manager at the startled pitcher. "But you're going, all right. Why, you dumb busher, if you pitched another no-hit game for me, I wouldn't have a player left! You're fired! Back to the bushes for you!"

☆ ☆ ☆